WONDERS OF MAN

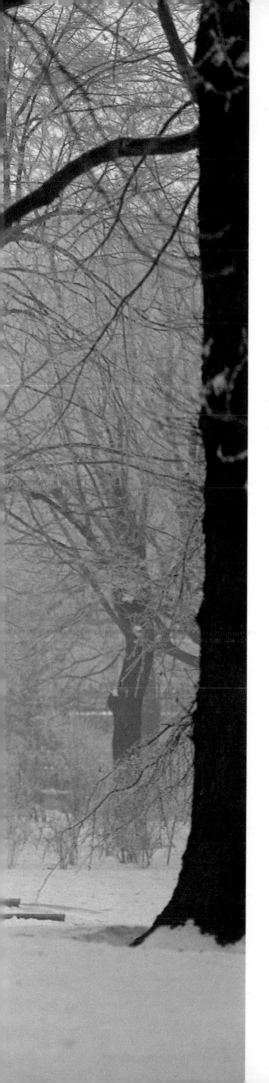

VIENNA

by Frederic V. Grunfeld

and the Editors
of the Newsweek Book Division

NEWSWEEK, New York

NEWSWEEK BOOK DIVISION

Edwin D. Bayrd, Jr.   *Editorial Director*
Henry A. La Farge   *Editor*
Mary Ann Joulwan   *Art Director*
Laurie P. Winfrey   *Picture Editor*
Eva Galan   *Assistant Editor*

Alvin Garfin   *Publisher*
William Urban   *General Manager*

WONDERS OF MAN

Milton Gendel   *Consulting Editor*

OPPOSITE: Visible from every part of the city, the great Gothic steeple of St. Stephen's Cathedral, built in 1433 and rising 450 feet, stands as an immutable symbol on the Vienna skyline. The squat tower to its left is the base of a corresponding steeple that was never built; it houses the famous Pummarin bell, cast from Turkish cannons in 1683.

TITLE PAGE: In the distinctive Burggarten park, bounded on two sides by the Hofburg, stands an equestrian statue of Francis I. After Napoleon's dissolution of the Holy Roman Empire, Francis became the first emperor of Austria. Then, after the fall of Napoleon in 1814, Francis presided over the Congress of Vienna—from which Austria emerged as the leading power in Europe.

Library of Congress Cataloging in Publication Data

Grunfeld, Frederic V.
Vienna.

(Wonders of man)
Bibliography: p.
Includes index.
1. Vienna (Austria)—History. I. Newsweek, inc.
Book Division. II. Title. III. Series.
DB847.G78   943.6'13   79-3538
ISBN 0-88225-304-2   AACR2

Printed and bound in Japan

Introduction

"Asia begins on the Landstrasse" is one of Prince Metternich's much-quoted epigrams. The Landstrasse runs from the center of Vienna through its eastern district, and indeed there have been epochs of Viennese history when "Asia" began just beyond the fortifications that once encircled the city.

The last time it happened was in 1683, when Vienna was besieged by nearly 300,000 Turkish troops under the Grand Vizier Kara Mustafa, the sultan's viceroy, who had dreams of establishing a western Muslim empire in the heart of Europe. For a time he seemed very close to fulfilling his plans. His soldiers swept across Hungary, aided by dissident Hungarian nobles who sided with the Turks against their liege lords, the Habsburgs. Kara Mustafa had reinforced his Turkish shock troops with allies and vassals from Asia Minor and North Africa—Kiabe tribesmen from Mesopotamia, Iraqis from Baghdad, Syrians from Aleppo and Damascus, Spahis from Morocco, Janissaries from Bulgaria and Greece, Vlachs from Rumania, Ukrainian Cossacks, Hungarians from Transylvania, and 14,000 Tartars. Thus one could look out from the ramparts of Vienna and see the whole of "Asia" drawn up in battle array.

At the eleventh hour the reigning Habsburg emperor, Leopold I, had decided to flee from Vienna together with his empress, then in the ninth month of pregnancy. They were joined in flight by 60,000 "men of all conditions," including most of the court officials. But General Starhemberg was left behind with a fighting force of 34,000 men and orders to hold the citadel. As the last refugees slipped out of the western gates, the Turkish vanguard was already moving into the city's eastern approaches. When their initial bombardment failed to breach the city's fortifications, Turkish sappers dug a series of mine-shafts under the bastion. It is said that one night the bakers' apprentices, hard at work on the next day's bread, heard peculiar noises and informed the Viennese garrison commander, who deduced that the enemy was driving a tunnel under the walls. He sank a counter-mine and blew the Turks out of theirs—and although the siege was to last another sixty days, Kara Mustafa never did succeed in taking the citadel.

The king of Poland, John Sobieski, had received "the bitter news of downtrodden Vienna" and went to the Austrians' rescue with an army of 30,000 men. They joined forces with the Habsburg troops under the Duke of Lorraine and defeated various elements of the Turkish force, some of whom had crossed the Danube and were cut off from the rest. In the end they fell on the vizier's camp, routed the main body of his army, and captured "27 flags, 22 standards, 36 camels and 600 horses." Even the bakers' apprentices were not left out of the victory celebrations that followed: by imperial decree, they baked a particularly tasty kind of bread, using milk and butter, which was formed into small loaves bent into the shape of the Turkish crescent or *croissant*, symbol of the defeated army and became an indispensable part of the Continental Breakfast.

This special knack for making the most of any situation—for filching the *croissant* from the enemy's banner—has always been the hallmark of Vienna's

genius for survival in a world fraught with dangers and complexities. Whenever the smoke clears after a crisis, Vienna emerges once again, having made suitable adjustments and absorbed whatever lessons could be learned from the experience.

Architecturally, too, Vienna has always been at its best when absorbing and transforming the impulses and influences that have come to it from the east and south, particularly the Moorish arches and Persian cupolas that were so smoothly integrated into the Viennese Baroque. The great palaces, churches, and monasteries that account for the city's architectural splendor all reflect something of this Eastern love of curves and arabesques, as though the Habsburg emperors had felt compelled to outshine their rivals, the Ottoman emperors.

This city, therefore, which once prided itself on being the easternmost bastion of Western power, has also served as a gateway by which Eastern ideas have entered the West. Vienna over the centuries became a meeting place of many cultures, interests, and traditions—a circumstance that gives modern Vienna a very special position among German-speaking cities. Its very raison d'être was that it lies on that great river highway, the Danube, just at the point where the natural routes from north to south cross those that lead from east to west. Here the river skirts the furthest spur of the alpine mountain system, and commences its long sweep southeast to the Black Sea. The last of the Alps defines its right bank; on the left stretches a vast plain reaching all the way to the Carpathians. The capitals of most other nations are somewhere near

the heart of the country, and thus geographically protected from attack; Vienna is perilously close to the periphery, exposed to every hostile wind that blows across the plain; the borders with both Czechoslovakia and Hungary are less than thirty miles away.

It seems a curiously vulnerable position from which to build a vast empire, yet the House of Habsburg did not miscalculate when it chose Vienna as the base from which to conduct its expansionist policies—an exercise in diplomacy and power politics that lasted from the thirteenth to the twentieth century. Like their later rivals, the Hohenzollern of Prussia, the Habsburgs had begun modestly enough with a single castle in southwest Germany, the Habichtsburg (Hawk's Castle) on the river Aar, near its junction with the Rhine. Circumstances played parts of Austria into their hands; they defended their holdings and acquired still more territory, not only by conquest and negotiation but also by marriage, giving rise to the oft-quoted Latin epigram, "*Bella gerant alii; tu, Felix Austria, nube*"— "Others make war; you, happy Austria, marry!"

This form of conquest-by-ingratiation produced such spectacular gains that, in the sixteenth century, the Habsburg emperor Charles V ruled not only over Austria, Styria, Carinthia, and Carniola, but also over Spain and the Spanish empire in America, the Netherlands, Sardinia, Naples and Sicily, the duchy of Milan, the Franche-Comté in France, and other desirable pieces of real estate too numerous to mention. By then, however, the Habsburg holdings had become too large for any one man to

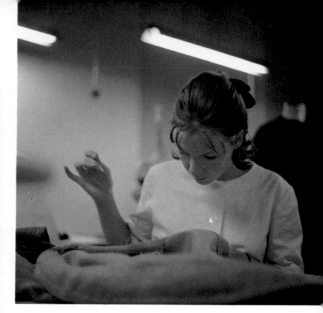

rule successfully, and Charles's inheritance was divided between the Spanish and the Austrian branches of the family.

Vienna became a great city, at any rate, partly because half of Europe was ruled from its royal palaces, and partly because the most talented and industrious people of this far-flung empire contributed to the civilization that was created here, layer upon layer and generation after generation. Alone among German-speaking cities, Vienna was on terms of intimate acquaintance with Brussels, Paris, Milan, Rome, Seville, Budapest, and Bucharest. In its halcyon days it was the only city in which the three main ethnic divisions of Europe—the Latin, the Teutonic, and the Slavonic—were represented by influential nobles as well as by important artists, poets, and musicians. The names of the great nobles who inhabited its palaces—Kinsky, Lobkowitz, Montenuovo, Pallavicini, Palffy, Esterházy, Czernin, Schwarzenberg, Liechtenstein—suggest the breadth of this ethnic spectrum, which included Germans, Czechs, Moravians, Ruthenians, Poles, Slovenes, Serbians, Croats, Italians, Romanians, and Magyars. In a sense, the Habsburg empire was the first of the multinational conglomerates, and it produced a cultural pluralism that seems all the more attractive when viewed from the vantage point of the late twentieth century. The narrow nationalisms that ultimately destroyed the empire have given rise to new nations (and endless political tensions) but nothing like the great flowering of culture that took place under the more or less enlightened egotism of the Habsburgs.

So long as Vienna remained the capital of this patchwork-quilt, fairytale kingdom, it continued to produce a marvelous series of cross-pollinated flowers. This was the city where Herr Mozart, from Salzburg, could collaborate with the Venetian poet, Lorenzo da Ponte, to create *Don Giovanni, The Marriage of Figaro,* and *Così Fan Tutte;* where Kapellmeister Joseph Haydn, from Rohrau in lower Austria, could spice his serenades with Croatian folk-dance rhythms; where Herr Beethoven, from Bonn (and of partly Flemish ancestry), could quote Russian folk-songs in his string quartets; where Johann Strauss the Elder, for once a native-born Viennese (the son of a baptized Jewish tavern-keeper from Budapest), composed the most vigorous of Czech polkas, where Johannes Brahms, from Hamburg, wrote quasi-authentic Hungarian dances; and where Gustav Mahler, from Kalischt (now Kaliste) in Bohemia, brought the Chinese pentatonic scale into the symphonic precincts of the concert hall.

As always when one wants to make a point about Viennese history, one is drawn back to its musical past. It is, as this book demonstrates, a city full of visual marvels, in architecture, sculpture, and painting. (Even today, in the Viennese school of so-called Magic Realists, it possesses the one clearcut movement in modern painting that is not merely a pale reflection of the New York School.) Still, there are other European cities that equal, or surpass, Vienna in museums, churches, palaces: Rome, Venice, and Florence; Paris, Prague, Moscow. In one respect, however, Vienna is unique among the wonders of man: it is the city of music par excellence.

Perhaps half or two-thirds of the important chapters in the history of classical music were written here, from the symphonies of Papa Haydn to the twelve-tone string quartets of Arnold Schoenberg and Anton von Webern. When Viennese guides take tourists through the city's palaces, they mention the builder, the architect, the year of construction, and so on—and then they add, "Haydn conducted the orchestra here," "Mozart played string quartets here," or "Beethoven improvised on this piano."

Vienna's instrumental music is a more vivid and permanent monument to its history than anything its sculptors have chiseled out of marble or cast in bronze. Each time the London Symphony, Tokyo Philharmonic, or Philadelphia Orchestra performs Mozart's "G Minor" or Beethoven's *Eroica*, it recreates, in immanent vibrations, an otherwise indefinable moment—a fragment of human consciousness lifted out of the past and brought back to life in the present. A work like *Don Giovanni* is a kind of time machine that can bring a perceptive listener far closer to the eighteenth century than any number of historical treatises, no matter how liberally strewn with footnotes.

A phenomenon like the Viennese cultural tradition is made up of countless intangibles: economic, social, and aesthetic. Still, at the crux of it is the relationship between artist and audience. There are epochs when "the time is right" for building exemplary structures like the Belvedere Palace. And once the palaces have been built the walls must be covered with paintings and tapestries. Then it is music's turn; no one could dream of dwelling in marble halls without the warming sounds of music to reverberate from those resonant walls. Suddenly there are new market opportunities—for sonatas, string quartets, serenades, symphonies. The owners and inhabitants of palaces are, to an astonishing extent, expert performers on stringed or keyboard instruments. Still, professionals must be brought in to make up the gaps in the chamber-music ensemble, and to supply the new music for which these wealthy amateurs have developed an insatiable appetite. A tradition is born, and with it a profession. Sometimes the great lords discover their household musicians among the peasants and retainers—as witness Joseph Haydn. More often they come from the growing class of musical functionaries, as did Bach, Mozart, and Beethoven. Where there is an established market for music, the supply will soon meet the demand.

It is hardly surprising that a society whose most gifted members could talk to one another in tones should have produced so many subtle and influential thinkers—Sigmund Freud, Otto Rank, and Alfred Adler among the psychologists; Fritz Mauthner, Ernst Mach, and Ludwig Wittgenstein in philosophy; Adolf Loos, Otto Wagner, and Josef Hoffmann among architects; and innumerable novelists, poets, playwrights, painters, critics, all of whom helped to usher in the so-called modern age. The revolution of perception in the arts that began with Beethoven's last string quartets was to reach fruition in Freud's *The Interpretation of Dreams* and Wittgenstein's *Tractatus Logico-Philosophicus*, both of which deal with the phenomena of language and

thought in wholly new dimensions. That final flowering of Vienna's *genius loci* also depended on the existence of a small elite audience that could perceive the importance of what was being said to it: circles of art lovers who bought Gustav Klimt's sinuous paintings and the shocking half-naked nudes of Egon Schiele; circles of psychoanalysts prepared to embark on the search for hidden meanings together with Freud, Adler, Rank, and company; circles of literati whose egotisms did not prevent them from listening very carefully, and with open minds, when a new voice wanted to make itself heard above the din.

By the end of the nineteenth century, as the emperor Franz Joseph's reign drew to a close, most residents were aware that the Habsburg empire was headed for bankruptcy and dissolution—yet it was at this very point that Viennese culture reached its apex. It was as though the phoenix had ascended before the fire. In retrospect, *fin-de-siècle* Vienna emerges as one of the great creative periods in the history of civilization—while, in the background, the old world raced toward disaster.

Time was running out for this extraordinary elitist civilization where, at the intellectual level, all the contrasts and conflicts between and among ethnic groups had been resolved in a spirit of harmonious coexistence reminiscent of the way Mozart had resolved the dissonances of his string quartets.

But while the Vienna of Karl Kraus and Hugo von Hofmannsthal did its utmost to forestall the catastrophe they sensed was coming, an underground movement of violence and hatred was already marshaling its forces. In turn-of-the-century Vienna, the best of modern civilization intersected with the worst. It was the city where Gustav Mahler, the greatest composer of the day and, by imperial decree, director of the Vienna Opera, was not permitted to conduct the municipal charity concerts because the burgomaster of Vienna, Carl Lueger (who had been elected on a virulently anti-Semitic platform), had instituted a policy of discrimination against Jews. In contrast to the tolerant world of the Habsburgs, there was the demagoguery of the Luegers and the racist parties; while humanists like Robert Musil, Alban Berg, Franz Werfel, and Oskar Kokoschka tried to bring about a millennium in the arts, the bully boys in the populist parties were preparing a revolution that was to do away with the whole of intellectual life. In that curious and sinister underworld, the young Adolf Hitler painted postcards and learned to hate his betters.

The work of destruction that began with World War I would thus be completed, twenty years later, by a vicious, ruthless political movement that sprang up like a deadly nightshade in the ruined gardens of the Habsburg empire. Misguided Viennese—and they included the great majority of "little men"— welcomed the Nazi Anschluss in 1938 with cries of joy and upraised arms. Admittedly, Hitler's popularity had faded considerably by the time Russian artillery zeroed in on the city in 1945—but only the nightmare of yet another invasion from the East was to release the city from its servitude. Not until it had undergone this new trial by fire could Vienna reemerge as one of the wonders of man.

VIENNA IN HISTORY

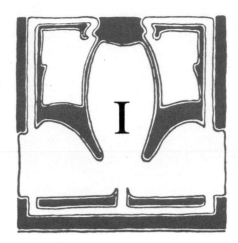

I

Among the traditional symbols of Vienna, the most imposing is the south tower of St. Stephen's Cathedral—a slim Gothic spire with a serrated silhouette, rising out of a cluster of slender buttresses and pointed arches near the center of the city. Built in the fourteenth century, the south tower rises to a height of 448 feet; it is the most important Gothic structure not only of Vienna but of all Austria, while the cathedral beside it, having been vandalized and lovingly restored countless times since the 1100s, is a remarkably unified collection of architectural styles from the Romanesque and the Gothic through the Baroque.

Looking down from this tower in 1841, the great Austrian essayist Adalbert Stifter observed the hundreds of people moving through the teeming city and compared it to a modern Babel. From the tower's highest window he could hardly see the streets themselves, only an astonishing mosaic of "roofs, gables, chimneys, towers, a confusion of prisms, cubes, pyramids, parallelepipeds, cupolas, as if they had all crystallized together. Indeed, seen from this bird's-eye perspective, the view has something adventurous and strange even for the native of Vienna, who hardly knows at first how to orient himself."

Now that there are high-rise buildings in the distance, the tower of St. Stephen has lost its monopoly of height, yet what Stifter wrote about the view from its window has lost none of its validity as a definition of the civilization responsible for erecting the tower, the cathedral, and the city itself.

Indeed, the cathedral and its soaring tower are a monument to the elasticity and perseverance of a culture that has withstood the vicissitudes of history and geography. This Babel of races, languages, and religions has absorbed a greater diversity of alien cultures than almost any other city of the Old World—settlers, invaders, traders, people who came for a visit and stayed for a lifetime. "If one falls, another is ready . . . to take his place." The conquerors and immigrants were drawn to Vienna because the site itself, this crossroads between East and West, possesses conditions favorable to the good life: the river, the soil, the climate.

People have lived in this region since the days of Neanderthal Man, first as nomadic hunters of the big game that migrated through the Danubian steppe during the Ice Age summers, later as settlers of the fertile lands adjoining the river. Judging from the prehistoric artifacts found in the area, the early residents developed an exceptionally high level of culture. The "Venus of Willendorf," a miniature stone figure of a mother goddess (now in the Vienna Museum of Natural History), was found in a village 4 miles from Vienna; it is one of the most remarkable relics of the great Stone Age tradition that flourished more than 20,000 years ago. She has a mass of tightly curled hair that any modern Viennese hairdresser would be hard put to equal, and a body consisting mainly of the intersecting melon shapes of her enormous breasts and buttocks. It is a powerful piece of sculpture, though she might be considered a rather corpulent Venus by *Vogue*-cover standards.

Even in this domain there is a sense of cultural

The Tower of Saint Stephen

continuity spanning all the millennia from the Stone Age to the present. The human needs and hopes embodied in the "Venus" are not so far removed from those that gave rise to the mother-goddess altars which existed here during the Roman empire and, after Christianity came to the Danube, to the countless shrines of the Madonna which are the pride of Catholic Vienna, and to which women who want children still make votive offerings.

The site on which Vienna is built, a large spur of land protected by a bend of the Danube, with a commanding view of the outlying plain, must have been a favorite camping and fishing ground from the very beginning. Its first known inhabitants, however, were the Celts, who established a settlement here about 500 B.C. and called it Vindomina, or "White Place." (The name is one of the longest-lasting of any European city, for Wien and Vienna are merely the result of mispronunciations or contractions of Vindobona, the Roman adaptation, by alien invaders of the Middle Ages.)

The first settlement's main reason for existence was that it lay on one of the major routes of the salt trade. The principal source of wealth among the Celts of this region was the salt mines of Hallstatt (the alpine settlement after which their civilization is named) and other mining areas of upper Austria and the Salzkammergut, the "salt-exchequer property" that lies between Salzburg ("salt castle") and Styria. Some of these salt deposits had been worked since paleolithic times, but the Celts displayed tremendous ingenuity and perseverance in getting the rock-salt out of the ground. They drove

tunnels more than 1,000 feet long into the mountains, where they worked at the salt-face by the light of pine torches and then hauled the salt up to the surface in leather backpacks.

Salt was one of the most precious trading commodities of ancient times, when many regions had no salt at all, and some parts of Germany had to make do with the ashes of certain kinds of saline wood. Every meal that included salt, the symbol of incorruption and perpetuity, was regarded as sacramental; a "covenant of salt" was one that could not be broken. But it was not only salt that passed through Vindomina on its way south and east. The golden amber of the Baltic and the North Sea—an even more precious and transportable commodity—traveled along the "amber road" from Jutland to Italy via the Semmering pass, or down to Greece and Asia Minor by way of the Danube.

The Celts were a people of great skill and energy; they introduced iron to central Europe, and with it the heavy plow tipped with an iron share that was to revolutionize agriculture in the Western world. Their works in bronze (to be seen in the Vienna Museum of Natural History) include some of the most striking pieces in the history of sculpture: jewelry, mythological figures, ritual vessels. Once the Roman empire began to expand northward, however, the days of Celtic autonomy were numbered. Roman legions conquered Vindomina in the early years of the Christian era, under the emperors Augustus and Tiberius. They changed the settlement's name to Vindobona and transformed it into a fortified camp from which to control the

Danube and protect their new province, Rhaetia, against invasion from the north.

Today, nothing survives of Roman Vindobona but a handful of museum pieces, a few references in the written record, and the catacombs beneath St. Stephen's Cathedral. Yet it was the Romans who created the urban core of Vienna—the shape of their defense lines was identical with that of the medieval city—and they were the first to exploit its strategic economic situation in the context of a "common market," that of the Roman empire. Vindobona had access to Byzantium by way of the Danube, which made it an ideal trading post for merchants from the inland provinces. Grain was carried from the Danube provinces to the Black Sea to feed the empire; a flotilla of river galleys and a system of watchtowers protected peaceful travelers against pirates and barbarians; and there was a regular service of ships from Ulm to the Black Sea, linking the Roman towns along the river.

A Roman road connected Rhaetia to Lake Constance and thence to Italy; by the second century A.D., Vindobona had become a *municipium* whose inhabitants enjoyed the rights of Roman citizens. Merchants from all corners of the known world came here to ply their wares—silks, spices, and other Oriental luxuries by way of Byzantium, pottery and olive oil from the western provinces, amber and walrus ivory from Scandinavia, exquisitely wrought jewelry from Scythia. Locally, the province produced not only salt but also gold and iron, and there was a rich variety of agricultural produce, including the clear, strong wine grown on the hill-

sides outside Vindobona. This wine-growing, wine-drinking tradition has remained a feature of Viennese life down the centuries and continues unabated in the *Heuriger*—literally, a "place where the new wine is served", a country-style tavern or restaurant of the sort that can now be found in the city itself as well as on the lower slopes of its rural hinterland, the Wienerwald.

Though Vindobona's garrison, one of the crack legions of the empire, had to be constantly on guard against barbarian incursions, life away from the front offered a rich variety of civilized pastimes. One could lounge at the hot springs at neighboring Baden ("bath") or attend the spectacles in nearby Carnumtum, whose amphitheater seated 13,000 spectators. The emperor Marcus Aurelius spent the better part of a decade here defending the frontier against the Marcomanni and their allies, the Quadi, and while he was campaigning he was setting down the "thoughts addressed to himself" now known as the *Meditations.* They were to establish his fame as a philosopher as well as his right to be considered the prophet of the true Viennese *esprit*—a profoundly pragmatic system of "living conformably to nature" in pursuit of tranquility, rendering to "body, soul, intelligence" that which naturally pertains to each: "to the body belong sensations, to the soul appetites, to the intelligence principles." Some 1,700 years later, another distinguished Viennese philosopher, Sigmund Freud, was to redefine these elements of the human psyche as the id, the ego, and the superego, but the essential concepts remained virtually identical.

Marcus Aurelius is thought to have died at Vindobona or at any rate nearby; the date was 180 A.D. He was better prepared for death than most other Roman emperors, for he had written, "Do not despise death, but be well content with it, since this too is one of those things which nature wills." The colonial system he helped create was to last until the fifth century, when the barbarians finally overran the imperial defenses, and the Roman legions abandoned Vindobona.

Successive waves of invaders, notably the Huns and the Avars, blotted out the written history of the place until the end of the eighth century. Yet legend and folklore insist that the town continued to thrive: Attila the Hun, "the scourge of God," was said to have set up his court there; and the seventh-century king Samo of the Slavs—almost as mythological a figure as his near-contemporary, King Arthur—is honored in oral tradition for having restored Vindobona to its former eminence as a commercial center. Charlemagne expelled the Avars toward the end of the eighth century and Vienna became a Carolingian-Frankish border fortress protecting the "Ostmark" (Eastern March) against attack. The record is unreliable, however, until the eleventh century, when Vienna is once again mentioned in medieval manuscripts.

At the time of the tenth-century emperor Otto II, the Ostmark was revived as a bulwark against the Magyars and was granted in fief to Leopold of Babenberg. Under the capable, enlightened rule of the Babenbergers, which was to last for 270 years, Vienna emerged from its dark age and witnessed a full-fledged renaissance. The town was rebuilt and fortified, commercial ties to Byzantium were reestablished, merchants and skilled tradesmen were granted tax privileges and other incentives designed to encourage the city's growth. The Magyar overlords had been driven out; and the Viennese now spoke German. Within a few generations, the German newcomers had been absorbed into the existing amalgam of nationalities produced by generations of invasions and occupations.

Vienna has remained an ethnic crucible ever since, for a "typical" Viennese may be the child of a Bavarian-Styrian father and a Slavic-Magyar mother; he may well marry a woman of Czech-Bohemian descent. The Babenbergers and other noble families intermarried just as readily, with the noble houses of Poland, Hungary, and Byzantium as well as those of Germany. Vienna also came to include the largest Jewish community in medieval Europe, thanks to fair-minded laws allowing them to engage in commerce and protecting them from gross persecution.

By the twelfth century Vienna had again become the main inland trade center between Europe and the Orient. As such it also served as an important way station on the overland route to the Crusades, supplying crusaders with provisions and equipment for the last stage of the journey to the Holy Land. In 1137 the town received the status of a *civitas*, and nineteen years later the Ostmark (Oesterreich, Austria) was advanced to the rank of a duchy under Duke Heinrich II (nicknamed "Jasomirgott" on account of the oath he was so fond of using—"So

help me God"). Heinrich moved his capital from a castle on what is now the Leopoldsberg, in the Vienna Woods, to the city itself. In the castle he built in what is now the square Am Hof not far from St. Stephen's, he and his successors maintained a lavish, cosmopolitan court that anticipated the city's later splendors. Such poets and musicians as the popular twelfth-century versifier from Kürenberg and the minnesinger Reinmar of Hagenau were drawn to Vienna by the Babenbergers' liberal patronage of the arts; foreign diplomats and nobles from the provinces would linger on at court long after their business had been concluded, attending tournaments and festivals of song.

It was the Babenbergers who created the basis for a new Austrian prosperity. They fortified the eastern and northern frontier with a chain of towers and castles; they encouraged the production and trade of gold, silver, and salt; and they established the first of the great monasteries that were to play a major role in the economic as well as religious and artistic development of Austria. An important monastery was founded at Melk in the year 1000, at Göttweig in 1074, and at Klosterneuburg in 1114.

With the functions of a capital added to those of fortress, commercial port, and religious center, the Vienna of the twelfth century soon expanded beyond the limits of the old Vindobona, which took up about half of the present inner city. At that time, most of the population lived in small one-story houses crowded together along streets that were even narrower than they are today, and burghers with growing families were obliged to build new

houses beyond the city walls. Even St. Stephen's, which was begun as a Romanesque parish church but soon overshadowed the older churches as the see of ecclesiastical authority in Vienna, was erected outside the then city wall, just beyond the southeastern corner of the old Roman ramparts.

Toward the end of the twelfth century, Duke Leopold V finally agreed to an extension of the walls and had his master builders construct most of the brick and earthwork defenses that would encircle the *Innere Stadt* until they were torn down in 1857 to make room for the Ringstrasse, the most fashionable street in modern Vienna. It is said that the duke financed this project, as well as the fortification of Wiener Neustadt, a garrison town he founded at a strategic site about 30 miles downriver, with the immense ransom he received for Richard Lion-Heart, an old enemy whom he caught trying to cross his domains incognito on the way home from the Third Crusade in 1192.

The enlarged city reached the peak of its medieval prosperity in the next generation, during the long reign of Leopold "the Glorious." Leopold earned his sobriquet thanks to impressive personal qualities and the talents of a statesman. He liked to entertain his subjects with jousting tournaments and court festivities, but he was also an eminently practical man, a sort of citizen-duke with a sure instinct for business and politics as well as a genuine concern for the welfare of his subjects. He stimulated trade by allowing merchants an even freer hand than they had previously enjoyed. Austria became the wealthiest duchy of the empire and Vienna—as Leopold

The great Benedictine Abbey of Melk, set on a promontory overlooking the Danube fifty miles upstream from Vienna, was originally a castle of the Babenberg overlords, predecessors of the Habsburgs. Toward the end of the eleventh-century it became a monastery, and in succeeding centuries it developed into a widely influential center of intellectual activity. Ruined in the Turkish invasion of 1683, the abbey was completely rebuilt between 1702 and 1726 in the exuberant Baroque style of the Counter Reformation. The magnificent interior of the abbey church (right), with its gilded statues and polychrome marbles, is dominated by the soaring main altar. The abbey's library (above) contains 100,000 books and manuscripts under a vaulted, frescoed ceiling. Equally splendid is the Court of the Prelates (below), with its elaborately sculptured ornamentation.

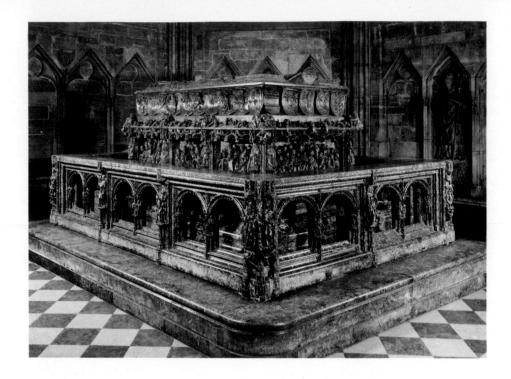

noted proudly—its chief city after Cologne.

As befitted so prosperous a community, Leopold inaugurated schools, commissioned his physician to open the city's first public hospital, and, most notably, conferred on the Viennese their earliest surviving charter. Dated 1221, it ranks among the most advanced legal codes of the epoch, and is comparable only to those of certain towns in England and Spain. Each burgher was accorded the right to inviolable privacy in his home—"which should be considered his castle"—and women had the right to marry as they wished and to inherit property. The city government was administered by councils of elected citizens, while the municipal judge (who also presided over the councils so as to prevent any serious threat to the duke's interests) was appointed by the duke.

Not all of Leopold's courtiers were happy with policies that narrowed the gap between the townsmen and the feudal aristocracy. Those who looked back nostalgically to the age of feudal privilege complained that a plebeian style had crept into the new Vienna, despite the superb new Gothic buildings and the splendor of its court. In music, for example—always an important reflection of the state of Viennese affairs—the duke's intimates preferred the four-square songs about nature and peasant life that people sang in the streets rather than the refined, elegant airs that had been cultivated by nobles of the previous generation. Aristocratic poet-composers like Walther von der Vogelweide, one of the great minnesingers (troubadours) in the old lyrical tradition and a favorite in Vienna until Leo-

pold's accession, could not bear the thought of joining this newly fashionable "croaking of frogs" and left the city to seek patronage from more conservative princes of the empire. He found other employers, but he was to have cause to complain in rhyme: *"lât iuch erbarmen, daz man mich bî sô rîcher kunst lât alsus armen"*—"A pity 'tis for sure, that a man so rich in art should have been kept so poor." Indeed, the great tradition of the troubadours was dying out all over Europe, soon to be replaced by the brilliant colors and seductive harmonies of early Renaissance music.

The Babenbergers were also about to disappear from the political stage. Leopold's son and heir, Frederick "the Quarrelsome," spent most of his sixteen-year reign waging unsuccessful wars of conquest against Hungary and Bohemia: he died childless in a battle against the former in 1246, leaving his domains open to conquest by the strongest pretender. At first the prize fell to King Ottocar Přemysl of Bohemia, but his territorial ambitions threatened both pope and emperor. The army of Rudolf von Habsburg, newly elected emperor of Germany, forced Ottocar to withdraw into Bohemia; when he reappeared with reinforcements in 1278, he was defeated and killed in a bloody battle on the Marchfeld—the same alluvial plain east of the city where Ottocar had earlier defeated the Hungarians.

The year 1278 is thus a decisive date in the history of Vienna and of Austria. Henceforth, until 1918, everything that happened to city and nation was to be intimately bound up with the destinies of a single great family, the Habsburgs, whose genius for aggrandizement is unmatched in the history of Europe. During the first two centuries of their rule they consolidated their position and extended their holdings to the south and west: Carinthia, Carniola, Styria, the Tyrol. . . .

Vienna soon reflected the growing power of its new rulers. The great tower of St. Stephen's, completed in 1439 after more than 150 years of Gothic enlargement and reconstruction of the old Romanesque church, was justly regarded as one of the technological marvels of the age: people came from far and wide to climb its 553 steps and look out over the unpolluted fifteenth-century landscape—literally a breathtaking view.

The tower served the Habsburgs as a symbol of the same lofty aspirations and imperial ambitions that are expressed in the ingenious motto whose initials appear on the tomb of Duke Frederick III in the cathedral itself: *A.E.I.O.U.*, standing for *Austria est imperare orbi universo*—"It is for Austria to rule the entire world." It was Frederick's son, Maximilian I, who commenced the Habsburgs' climb to worldwide importance in 1477 by marrying Mary, daughter and heiress of Charles the Bold of Burgundy, who brought him vast holdings in France and the Lowlands, including some of the richest lands in Europe. Maximilian ranks as the "second founder" of the house of Habsburg, not only because he acquired Burgundy and Flanders, but because he created a powerful legend of imperial glory. His courage and intelligence, scholarship and sensitivity would have made him an outstanding

Rudolfus Rex Romanorum primus

ruler in an age of absolutism had he not been headstrong and impulsive. As it was, his troubled reign as Holy Roman Emperor produced a long series of military reverses and fiascos, in France, Italy, Bavaria, Switzerland, the Lowlands.

Yet "Kaiser Max" became a German folk hero—because he, more than any other man of his time, understood the art of managing the news and manipulating what are now known as "the media." He commissioned painters, sculptors, poets, and musicians; he enlisted the services of specialists in the newly invented art of printing; he supported universities and various scholarly enterprises, such as the copying of old manuscripts and collecting of medieval poems; he was fond of dancing, jousting, hunting, and fishing—he wrote a *Hunt Book* purporting to teach his grandsons the art of hunting, and a *Fishing Book,* describing all the fishes to be found in the provinces of Austria. Albrecht Dürer created a paper Arch of Triumph for him, a *Triumphbogen* 11 feet high and 10 feet wide, printed with 109 separate woodcuts. Other artists celebrated his largely imaginary triumphs in a painted and printed *Triumphzug*—a splendid cycle of 137 woodcuts and 109 miniature paintings illustrating an imaginary Roman-style triumphal procession. It is one of the great works of Renaissance Europe, and the fact that it depicts a purely fictitious event makes it no less remarkable. Among other things, the paper procession contains one of the earliest accurate representations of an elephant in European art; Hans Burgkmaier used it to illustrate the idea, then wholly fanciful, that Maximilian had "brought

MAXIMILIANVS. I. IMP.
ARCHIDVX AVSTRIÆ
DVX BVRGVNDIÆ

PHILIPPVS HISP. REX. I.
ARCHIDVX AVSTRIÆ.

MARIA DVCISSA
BVRGVNDIÆ MAX: VXOR.

FERDINANDVS. I. IMP.
ARCHIDVX AVSTRIÆ

CAROLVS. V. IMP.
ARCHIDVX AVSTRIÆ.

LVDOVICVS. REX
HVNG MAS.

29

beneath our empire's yoke / the far-off Calcuttish folk.''

What was only a dream for Maximilian became reality for his grandson and successor, the emperor Charles V, who joined the traditional Habsburg lands in central Europe to the vast international domains of his maternal grandparents, Ferdinand and Isabella of Spain, and thereby ruled over an empire on which "the sun never set." Actually governing these far-flung territories, however, was a complex matter in an age of horseback and sail-driven communication. When Charles assumed full power in 1519—he was not yet nineteen—he found an empire already too large to rule alone. Not long afterward he split his legacy in two, keeping Spain for his own line and ceding the Austrian dominions to his younger brother Ferdinand, who was eventually to succeed to the crown of the empire as well. Ferdinand also followed another family tradition: he acquired Hungary and Bohemia through his marriage to the heiress of these two kingdoms, the princess Anna Jagiello.

Ferdinand's Spanish upbringing and the close ties maintained between the two Habsburg branches added yet another foreign ingredient to the Viennese melting pot. Court life acquired an air of southern *grandeza,* with dashing *caballeros* galloping about on the Glacis—a parade ground outside the city walls—on their magnificent Spanish-Arabic stallions. Their style of horsemanship can still be seen, essentially unaltered, at the Sunday-morning performances of *Haute École* riding presented at the Spanish Riding School in a corner of the Hofburg.

Ferdinand I, his son Maximilian II, and their descendants were avid art collectors. Their lavish purchases provided the nucleus for the truly royal collections now housed in the Kunsthistorisches Museum—paintings by Dürer, Rubens, Rembrandt, the Brueghels, van Dyck, Memling, Roger van der Weyden, Velazquez, Titian, Correggio, Perugino, Raphael, Andrea del Sarto. . . . The great nobles of the realm followed their example by building increasingly sumptuous palaces and forming superb collections of their own. The princes of Liechtenstein, to take only one famous example, amassed a magnificent private collection rich in Rubens and van Dyck in addition to priceless Italian pictures by Raphael, Botticelli, and Leonardo da Vinci (whose portrait of Ginevra dei Benci was sold by the present prince of Liechtenstein to the National Gallery in Washington, D.C., for a reputed $7 million).

Of course Vienna's emergence as a city of imperial splendor did not take place without setbacks and disasters. During the late Middle Ages there were fires, floods, earthquakes, the Black Plague. (The Jews were blamed for these catastrophes, stripped of their civil rights, and ultimately banished.) On the eastern front, the powerful Ottoman empire expanded through Hungary to within 70 miles of Vienna. In 1529 their first attack was beaten off, but the Turkish menace would remain constant until they were finally defeated after the memorable siege of 1683. The Turks, moreover, severed the lucrative trade routes to the Orient, causing a precipitous decline in the Viennese economy. Mean-

In the celebrated sequence of 137 woodcuts by Hans Burgkmair and other artists depicting the **Triumph of Maximilian I,** *the centerpiece is Albrecht Dürer's engraving of the emperor and Mary, the heiress of Burgundy, on a ceremonial chariot (below). Emulating the practice of Roman emperors, who glorified victories through triumphal processions, Maximilian commissioned this remarkable graphic series to broadcast the great events and accomplishments of his reign. Each plate represents a subject specified by Maximilian. For the group shown at left, for example, he stipulated "After them shall come on horseback Burgundian fifers in the Burgundian colors with bombardons, shawns and reed pipes. And they shall be wearing laurel wreaths."*

The rebuilding of Vienna with Baroque palaces and churches following the defeat of the Turks in 1683 reached a monumental peak in the Court Library (left), erected in 1722. With its magnificent frescoed dome and barrel-vaulted bays, it is the crowning achievement of the German-born architect Johann Bernhard Fischer von Erlach, who was trained in Rome by Bernini, the greatest exponent of the Baroque. The library is the perfect expression of Vienna as imperial capital, and revives the concept of dynastic world power inaugurated by Charlemagne. RIGHT: Seldom has Baroque sculpture reached such apocalyptic expression as in the Plague Monument, erected by Leopold I as a memorial to the 70,000 Viennese who died in the cholera epidemic of 1679. The standing figure with cross at the base of the monument calls on divine mercy to relieve the agony.

while, after the onset of the Reformation, the predominantly Protestant Viennese entered a long, losing struggle with their Habsburg overlords, who were determined to uphold the Catholic faith and to stamp out heresy throughout the empire. Ferdinand's accession in 1558 inaugurated an era of religious repression that was to last for more than a century before Catholicism was fully restored; those who refused to conform were burned at the stake or forced to join the mass migrations to the Protestant lands of northern Germany. At the same time the Habsburgs reestablished their rule as absolute monarchs, abrogating the city charter and filling municipal posts with their own appointees, obedient and very rank-conscious civil servants who gradually erected the top-heavy structure of bureaucrats that was to become a notorious feature of Viennese life and is still powerful today.

Despite the curtailment of their freedoms, the Viennese stubbornly preserved their pride behind a mask of politeness and urbanity. They remained prosperous enough to vent their frustrations by seizing every possible opportunity for feasting, drinking, and making music. Abraham a Sancta Clara, a monk from Swabia who moved to Vienna in 1662 and became the city's most famous preacher, rebuked the Viennese for being two-faced and denounced them from the pulpit for producing "false talk, false writing, false coin, false wines, false gold, false silver, false flowers, false jewelry, false hair, false friends." Even in the face of expected disaster, on the eve of the Great Plague of 1679, the city's "ringing trumpets and music resounding

everywhere . . . made such a noise that it was as if a hole had opened in the sky and joy were being poured down in the city by the bushel." It was, indeed, very difficult to prevent the Viennese from enjoying themselves even under the most adverse conditions.

Vienna remained on the front line, in effect, until the Turks were finally driven off in 1683: only then did the city's builders feel sufficiently safe to realize their dream of expanding their architectural horizons beyond the confinement of the old ramparts. It is an ill wind that blows nobody any good: Turkish bombardment had caused widespread damage and thus provided a welcome opportunity to build new palaces within the city as well. The nobles' newly acquired sense of security and space found expression in the great Baroque building boom that, within a few decades, transformed Vienna from a fortress city into an imperial capital that was the pride of central Europe. Splendid palaces and villas, churches and monasteries sprang up everywhere, as the nobles of the court engaged in a flurry of competitive building. The Liechtensteins, Althars, Orsinis, Batthyanys, Schwarzenbergs—and others of the eighty great families, from every part of the empire, who dominated the social scene—commissioned winter palaces in the city and summer residences on the outskirts. Needless to say they vied with one another at every turn, whether it was to produce the most elegantly proportioned façade, the most sumptuous living quarters, or the most exotic formal garden. Building was "a devilish passion," conceded Count Schönborn, the imperial vice

33

In regal recompense for his final victory over the Turks at
Zenta in 1697, Prince Eugene of Savoy was granted a tract
of land outside the city walls by the emperor Charles VI.
Commissioning the architect Lucas von Hildebrandt, Prince
Eugene built not one but two palaces, separated by a parterre
of formal gardens. The Lower Belvedere (foreground)
was erected in 1714 as a residence; the huge Upper Belvedere
(background), in 1721, for royal entertainment on a grand
scale. Acquired by the empress Maria Theresia after Eugene's
death, the latter palace has been the site of state functions
until the present day. In the resplendent Baroque interior of
marble and gilded decoration (left) stands the **Apotheosis of
Prince Eugene,** an allegorical marble group commissioned by
the prince himself from Balthasar Permoser

chancellor whose "Italian villa" in the suburbs was regarded as a model of tasteful magnificence, "but once you have started you cannot stop."

The Belvedere Palace, completed in 1723 as a summer residence for Prince Eugene of Savoy, stands out as a particularly striking example of Viennese Baroque architecture. Built by the famous architect Lucas von Hildebrandt in the Italianate style then in fashion, it contains more than 1,000 lavishly appointed rooms and boasts an immense fairytale garden with sculptured fountains and Elysian promenades in which to while away an enchanted afternoon. The palace occupies a commanding position on a tract of land which the emperor Charles VI bestowed on Eugene of Savoy—his *generalissimus* in the brilliant victory over the Turks at Zenta in 1697—as a mark of special favor. History continued to be made here long after Eugene's death: Maria Theresia acquired the property from his successors; the engagement of her daughter Marie Antoinette to the future king of France was celebrated here. Napoleon's officers admired the Belvedere when he conquered the city; later, during the Congress of Vienna, many of the royal delegates could be seen skating on a pond in its gardens. The student revolutionaries of 1848 set up their headquarters here; Anton Bruckner worked on his ninth symphony within its walls; it was from here that the Archduke Franz Ferdinand, heir to the throne, set off for the fateful visit to Sarajevo that was to spark off World War I. In 1955 the state treaty restoring sovereignty to Austria was signed here; in 1980 the foreign ministers of the signatory powers met here to celebrate the treaty's anniversary, and to search for new ways of preserving the peace of Europe. . . . In Vienna, history tends to happen in Baroque frames, even when the prevailing style is art nouveau or Bauhaus Modern.

Another of the great monuments of the age, not far from the Belvedere, is the church of St. Charles Borromeo, designed by Hildebrandt's great rival, Johann Bernhard Fischer von Erlach, for Charles VI. Many architectural historians consider this church, with its Corinthian portico and soaring oval dome, the finest example of the Viennese Baroque. But not to be forgotten is Fischer's other masterpiece, the palace of Schoenbrunn, originally begun in 1690s Baroque for the emperor Leopold I (Fischer was court architect as well as the tutor of the emperor's son) but completed and decorated in 1740s Rococo by Maria Theresia, who summoned artists from every part of Europe to provide the décor for this favorite among her palaces.

Visitors to Vienna during the years following the Turkish siege marveled at this city of palaces and churches that had materialized so suddenly on the edge of the Danubian plain. One especially articulate foreigner who kept a record of her impressions was Lady Mary Wortley Montagu, wife of an English diplomat sent to conduct negotiations at the imperial court in 1716. "I must own that I never saw a place so perfectly delightfull as the Fauxbourgs of Vienna," she wrote in one of her letter-essays on the city. "It is very large and almost wholly compos'd of delicious Palaces; and if the Emperor

OVERLEAF: Bernardo Bellotto's View of Vienna from the Belvedere *is one of thirteen cityscapes commissioned by the empress Maria Theresia during the Venetian artist's 1759–1760 visit. Seen from a balcony in the northwest corner of the Upper Belvedere, the palace grounds slope toward the city. St. Stephen's spire at center and the Karlskirche at left intersect the rising ground of the Vienna Woods in the distance. At right, the Salesian Nunnery overlooks the formal gardens and fountains of the Belvedere, peopled with promenaders. Between the Schwarzenberg Palace at left center and the Karslkirche open space extends to the city walls. A century later, when Vienna's old fortifications were torn down, this space became the Ringstrasse.*

found it proper to permit the Gates of the Town to be laid open that the Fauxbourgs might be joyn'd to it, he would have one of the largest and best built Citys of Europe. Count Schonbourne's Villa is one of the most magnificent, the Furniture all rich brocards, so well fancy'd and fited up, nothing can look more gay and splendid, not to speak of a Gallery full of raritys . . ."

In the inner city the streets were too narrow and crowded for her taste, particularly since they made it impossible to stand back and observe the majestic façades of the town palaces. Yet once inside, "nothing can be more surprizingly magnificent than the Apartments. They are commonly a suitte of 8 or 10 large rooms, all inlaid, the doors and windows richly carv'd and Gilt, and the furniture such as is seldom seen in the Palaces of sovereign Princes in other Countrys: the Hangings the finest Tapestry of Brussells, prodigious large, looking glasses in silver frames, fine Japan Tables, the Beds, Chairs, Canopys and window Curtains of the richest Genoa Damask or Velvet, allmost cover'd with gold Lace or Embroidery—the whole made Gay by Pictures and vast Jars of Japan china, and almost in every room large Lustres of rock chrystal."

During the great palace-building boom, people at the middle and lower levels of Viennese society also prospered. Streams of masons, carpenters, roofers, and other specialists poured into the city, together with sculptors, painters, and architects. The profits of the furniture makers and the damask dealers enriched the local industries; Vienna became an affluent society. One typical Baroque suc-

cess story is that of Franz Koltschitzky, a hero of the siege whose knowledge of Turkish had allowed him to pass through the enemy lines in order to carry an urgent message to the allied forces. When the municipal authorities asked him what he would like by way of reward, he requested the sacks of coffee beans which the fleeing Turks had left behind in their camp. He was also granted a tax-free house on the Singerstrasse, a stone's throw from the cathedral. Here he opened the "Blue Bottle," the city's first *Kaffeehaus*; it had six marble-topped tables, four benches, six chairs, a large mirror, and a portrait of the emperor Leopold hanging on the wall. Koltschitzky offered a dark, thick Turkish coffee with milk or cream, house copies of the *Wienerisches Diarium,* and an unhurried atmosphere—an immediately successful formula that was soon copied by other establishments and remains the *Kaffeehaus* ideal to this day.

By 1740, when the twenty-three-year-old Maria Theresia ascended the throne, Vienna had undergone an almost total renewal. The cathedral of St. Stephen, the old ramparts around the inner city, and a few other important relics of the Middle Ages remained as anchors in the past, but the queen's grandfather, Leopold, would have recognized very little of his old capital. Though its population was still less than 200,000, it was considered one of the most beautiful cities of Europe, a royal metropolis capable of attracting the finest minds and most creative spirits of an empire that stretched from the North Sea to the Adriatic, and from France to Turkey.

During the spring of 1745, the young queen-empress Maria Theresia decided to spend the *Pfingsten* (Whitsun) holiday at her summer palace, Schoenbrunn, and she ordered the choir boys of St. Stephen's Cathedral to join her court orchestra and choir in providing music for the occasion. Schoenbrunn had been left unfinished under Charles VI, who had run out of money, and it was now being reconstructed: the Italian architect Nicolas Pacassi had been commissioned to adapt Fischer von Erlach's plans to the prevailing Rococo taste for lighter, more airy buildings.

When the choir boys had finished singing they discovered the scaffolding that had been erected by the builders; it offered an irresistible invitation to young climbers and acrobats. They swarmed up the ladders and, in the words of one account, "made a lot of noise playing around on the boards." Suddenly a stern young woman appeared on the scene—Maria Theresia herself. She ordered one of her aides to remove the boys from the scaffolding; if anyone tried it again he was to be given a good beating. Next day one of the boys did do it again, was promptly caught, and received the promised thrashing. The empress demanded of her choirmaster, Georg Reutter, who that "fair-haired idiot" was—but not until many years later did she learn that he was one of the two most gifted musicians of her realm, Franz Joseph Haydn. It was Haydn himself who told her the story in 1773, when she paid a formal visit to the glittering country palace of Esterháza, where Haydn served as music director to Prince Nikolaus Esterházy, alias "Nikolaus-the-lover-of-Magnificence" (*der Prachtliebende*).

This formidable nobleman and patron of the arts was not only a field marshal in the Austrian army but also the richest man in the empire—wealthier, indeed, than the empress herself. It was understandable that she should have been impressed and delighted by the superb entertainment the prince staged in her honor, especially by the music that Haydn composed and conducted for her. Nikolaus received her royal thanks, but Haydn, the "fair-haired idiot" now grown to musical eminence, received a golden snuffbox filled with ducats.

The prince had spared no effort or expense to make his summer palace, 40 miles from Vienna, a "Hungarian Versailles," and since this was the empress' first visit to the newly completed Schloss Esterháza, he was determined to put his best foot forward. The program of festivities with which he welcomed his sovereign is a perfect expression of that fascination with all things musical and theatrical which was one of the ruling passions of the age. Though the visit lasted for only two days, it included an orchestral concert at which Haydn conducted the première of a new symphony, entitled "Maria Theresia," that he had composed in her honor, as well as a Haydn puppet opera, *Philemon und Baucis,* which concluded with an allegory designed to warm the empress' heart: the armorial bearings of the Habsburgs appeared among the clouds, surrounded by a halo and supported by the figures of Truth, Wisdom, and Gentleness, while Fame held a crown above them and puppets clad in Hungarian costumes, representing Obedience, Devotion, and

A Little Night Music

Loyalty, were kneeling and singing the empress' praises. These, of course, were no ordinary puppets, but the finest, most splendidly appointed set of Italian *fantocci* (marionettes) in the whole of northern Europe. Later that evening there was a fancy dress ball in Prince Esterházy's new "Chinese Pleasure House"—a ballroom 130 feet long, filled with treasures of chinoiserie, its mirrored walls reflecting the light of 600 candles. Finally there was a giant pyrotechnic display designed by a master of fireworks, followed by mass folk-dancing in honor of the royal guest—a thousand peasants in Hungarian and Croatian folk costumes, dancing to their own bands. They symbolized the pleasures of country living as distinct from those of the capital. Legally, indeed, they were light years removed from Vienna, since the Hungarian peasants were still serfs, while those just across the river, in Austria, were free.

Haydn, who spent two or three months a year in Vienna and the rest at Esterháza or the prince's other main residence, in Eisenstadt, was happy enough with the musical independence he enjoyed as director of music for an establishment that included, besides the marionettes, an opera house, a theater for comedies, and an orchestra of virtuosos who also performed church and chamber music. "My prince was satisfied with all my works," he explained after his retirement. "I was applauded, and as director of an orchestra I could make experiments and observe what makes an impression and what detracts from it; I could improve my music, add to it, make cuts, and be as bold as I pleased. I was cut off from the world, there was no one

to confuse or torment me, and I was forced to become original."

In other respects, however, he preferred life in the city to his isolated and rather spartan existence in the country. In later years he would write plaintive letters to his Viennese friends telling them how much he had enjoyed his visit to the capital. "Well—here I sit in my wilderness—forsaken—like a poor waif—unhappy," he wrote to his music-loving confidante, Maria Anna von Genzinger, in 1790. He wished he could be back at the "wonderful parties" she had given, "where the whole circle is of one heart, one soul. All these beautiful musical evenings—which can only be remembered, not described. . . ."

The reasons why Vienna became the cynosure of musicians were not unconnected with the *joie de vivre* and receptivity to new influences that also manifested themselves in Viennese cuisine. The ragout was French, the pastry Danish, the pineapple came from the Spanish possessions in the New World, the coffee from Turkey. . . . Haydn's music was rooted in a comparable spectrum of cultures. His orchestral and chamber music contains countless quotations from old Slavonic and Balkan folk songs, including "the march which is commonly played in Turopol at rustic weddings," and all kinds of Hungarian tunes, by no means all of them marked *rondo all 'Ongharese.* There were also Russian influences, as well as Spanish, Italian, and French; in later years he was even to compose music to English texts for British audiences.

Next to London, Vienna was certainly the most

cosmopolitan city in Europe, and it became famous for possessing the wealthiest, most influential, and most dedicated colony of music lovers, beginning with the emperors themselves. The Habsburgs had been musical for generations, and not just in a superficial way. Leopold I, emperor during the Turkish siege, had composed a large amount of thoroughly professional church music, including masses, oratorios, and cantatas: as the Marshal de Gramont once noted, "his only pleasure consists of composing sad music." Joseph I, who played flute and harpsichord, wrote arias and passion music in the style of George Frederick Handel. Charles VI used to lead the court orchestra from his seat at the harpsichord, "displaying on that instrument the eminent skill of a professor." When the court *Kapellmeister* ventured to congratulate him on his accomplishments—"It is a pity that Your Majesty did not choose to become a virtuoso!"—Charles replied, in his dry humor, "Never mind, I get a better break this way!"

Maria Theresia, the beautiful crown princess who had to play a man's role in politics because there was no male heir to the throne, nevertheless excelled in the ladylike art of singing soprano arias. She made her debut as a singer at the age of five; at twenty-two, on a visit to Florence, she sang a duet with Senesino (Francesco Bernardi, one of the most famous singers of the day) that "so captivated the old man . . . that he could not proceed without shedding tears of satisfaction." Her son and heir, Joseph II, was trained as a bass in the Italian school, and played viola, cello, and harpsichord, usually

as accompanist to the singers whom he invited to his musicales. He was in the habit of making music for an hour after dinner every evening, and three times a week there was a private concert involving the leading court musicians; he himself always played, but no outsiders were invited to hear these royal performances.

All of Maria Theresia's children were brought up as musicians. She and Francis I had five sons and eleven daughters, ten of whom survived her. One of her nobles remembered seeing four archduchesses of Austria, the royal princesses, "appear at court in the opera *Egeria,* written by Metastasio and set by Hasse, expressly for their use. They were then extremely beautiful, sung and acted very well for princesses, and the grand duke of Tuscany [their brother], who was likewise very handsome, danced, in the character of Cupid."

It was, even in a musical age, a court that went to extraordinary lengths to cultivate opera and chamber music. And by the same token, the professionals they employed to write their music and texts were artists of the first rank. Johann Adolf Hasse was one of the many north German composers who came to Vienna in search of a living. He wrote vast quantities of music—so much, in fact, that he admitted that he would not recognize many of his pieces if he heard them again—but all of his manuscripts were burned during the bombardment of Dresden, so that little is left of his life's work. It was all the fault of Frederick the Great, another music-loving monarch, who took advantage of Maria Theresia's rather tenuous right to rule

by despoiling her empire of its cloth-weaving province of Silesia. During the Seven Years' War, en route to Silesia, Frederick's artillery set fire to Dresden, and with it the manuscripts that Hasse had assembled there in preparation for a complete edition of his works. Yet Hasse never bore Frederick a grudge, for he was convinced that the king would have altered his strategy, or at least delayed the bombardment, had he realized what a loss to music it was going to inflict. "If His Majesty had known that contingencies would have obliged him to bombard Dresden, he would previously have apprised me of it, that I might have saved my effects!" In 1760, if there was anything more important than a military victory, it was the score to a good opera.

Pietro Metastasio, who wrote librettos for Hasse and for dozens of other composers, held the post of Austrian court poet for fifty years. He was one of the most brilliant Italian poets of the century, but no one thought it strange that he should make his home in Vienna rather than in Rome. Haydn, as a very young man, lived in the attic of the house where Metastasio occupied an apartment on the fourth floor; the elderly poet befriended the young musician, who had just been expelled from St. Stephen's choir with yet another beating—for having cut off a fellow chorister's pigtail during a performance. As Stendhal wrote in his *Letters on Haydn*, "Metastasio, dining every day with Haydn, gave him some general rules respecting the fine arts; and, in the course of his instructions, taught him Italian." It was one of the happy features of Vienna that chance encounters of this kind were constantly taking place, adding new and unforeseen elements to the city's cultural alloy. What Haydn learned from Metastasio he afterward put to good use writing Italian operas for the Esterházys, in which he combined his own particular genius for instrumental music with the vocal brilliance of the Italian tradition. He had learned more about the latter from Niccolò Porpora, a friend of Metastasio's and one of the leading Italian composers of the "old school." Porpora had come to Vienna on a mission of some delicacy—he had been engaged as singing master to the mistress of the Venetian ambassador. Haydn, in turn, was hired as accompanist for the lady's singing lessons. "I was called all sorts of names, *asino, coglione, birbante,* and given many a cuff in the ribs, but I let him do as he pleased, for I learned a great deal from Porpora in singing, composition and the Italian language."

Haydn—the son of a cartwright and of a cook in the service of Count Harrach, the eldest son of his father's seventeen children—was penniless at the time. To keep body and soul together he gave music lessons, sang in church choirs, and, in the evening, "he would often go *gassatim* with his musical comrades"—that is, he was hired by affluent amateurs to make up the serenading parties that went round the streets and alleys (*Gassen*) of Vienna, playing serenades, *cassations* (*Gassen*-pieces), *notturnos,* and the like.

The profusion of special names for various kinds of serenades testifies to the importance of this kind of music-making in the rococo scheme of things. The word *serenata,* for that matter, derives from

The central figure in the creation of classical music in eighteenth-century Vienna was Franz Joseph Haydn (left). After singing in the choir of St. Stephen's, where he received his principal training, he had the advantage of serving for almost thirty years as musical director in Prince Nikolaus Esterházy's glittering country palace outside Vienna, an establishment that included an opera house, a theater for comedies, and an orchestra that performed church and chamber music. In Vienna, Haydn made the early acquaintance of a brilliant Italian poet, Pietro Metastasio (right), who wrote librettos for the Austrian court and taught Haydn Italian, enabling him to write Italian operas for Esterházy, and introducing him to the Italian tradition of improvised street serenading. Out of these varied strands the fabric of Haydn's music was woven.

"serenity," and not, as some suppose, from *sera,* the Italian word for evening. A *notturno,* on the other hand (such as Haydn later wrote for the king of Naples), is music specifically written to be played at night. The *Ständchen,* a German term that Franz Schubert preferred, is "a little stand-up piece" for people singing or playing on their feet. The *divertimento* is a musical diversion, as the name implies, appropriate either indoors or out, but the *Feldpartie* and the *concert champêtre* are definitely country cousins, intended to be played at open-air fêtes and lawn parties that took place at the hunting lodges and *Jagdschlösser* where the nobility disported themselves. Mozart headed his most famous serenade with a deceptively simple descriptive title: "*Eine kleine Nachtmusik*"—"a little night music."

But serenading was only one of the Viennese ways of weaving music into the pattern of daily life. The English musical traveler, Dr. Charles Burney, who came to Vienna in 1772, was amazed to see a Sunday-morning procession, two or three miles long, "singing a hymn to the Virgin, in three parts, and repeating each stanza after the priests, in the van, at equal distances; so that the instant one company had done, it was taken up by another behind, till it came to the women in the rear, who, likewise, at equal distances, repeated, in three parts, the few simple notes of this hymn; and even after them it was repeated by girls, who were the last persons in the procession." It seemed to Dr. Burney, indeed, that this city, with its addiction to music and large number of composers "of superior merit," deserved to rank as, "among German cities, the imperial seat of music, as well as of power."

At the other end of the cultural scale there were the formal concerts and operatic performances that took place in the palaces of the great nobles. At the Habsburgs' city residence, the Hofburg, at Schoenbrunn, and in the Belvedere, the Redoutensaal, the *palaix* of the Hungarian magnates and Bohemian princes, the air reverberated more or less continually with the sound of music. The real *genius loci* of Vienna revealed itself in these activities, for the paintings and tapestries on the walls were apt to be the product of Italy, France, or Flanders; only the music was largely homemade. And it was Haydn who first pulled together the several strands of this rich and heterogeneous tradition in order to weave them into the remarkable musical tapestry now known as Viennese Classicism. His style and method owed a great deal to his diverse experiences as a choir boy and operatic accompanist, as a midnight serenader and orchestral *Kapellmeister.*

Admittedly, "classical" is a curious term for the music of an epoch that, at least visually, has so little in common with the purity of line usually associated with classical antiquity. Architecturally, the background to Viennese classical music—the shell- and scrollwork decorations, the endless draperies and arabesques—seems anything but Hellenic in its inspiration. The music, however, is far more direct and to the point than the architecture; it borrows the brilliance of the Baroque, but discards its polyphonic intricacies in order to focus on the expressive potential of melody, raised to the nth power by means of new harmonic procedures. Haydn's

In the great hall of the Spanish Riding School (above), a masterpiece of Baroque architecture by Fischer von Erlach, the empress Maria Theresia staged a spectacular carousel of court ladies with swords drawn, riding on horseback or seated in carriages, to celebrate the Austrian victory over Frederick the Great in 1757. Equestrian performances in the Riding School continue to this day (left). Horses of the famous Lippizaner breed, introduced from Spain in the sixteenth century, are trained at the school in amazingly intricate haute école *movements. Here, a horse and its rider are performing the soaring leap called the* capriole.

symphonies and string quartets are "classical" in the more basic sense, in that they establish models and methods which the composers who came after him considered "classicall and canonicall."

By modern standards, the "Viennese classical" orchestra was hardly more than a skeletal organization. Haydn's orchestra at Esterháza consisted of only eleven violins, himself included, and two each of violas, cellos, contrabassos, bassoons, and horns, with trumpets and drums available on call, if necessary, from the prince's military guard. Yet this was the organization for which Haydn wrote the vast majority of the 107 symphonies that establish his reputation as "the father of the symphony." Only gradually, as he was "forced to become original," did he evolve the immensely versatile, dynamic forms that were to dominate the next century and a half of music-making, not only in Austria but throughout the world of Western "classical" music.

What Haydn labored a lifetime to accomplish, Mozart acquired intuitively and almost without effort. Wolfgang Amadeus Mozart was the other pillar on which Viennese classicism rests. He was twenty-four years younger than Haydn, who regarded him as "the greatest musical genius that ever existed"—"a *god* in music." It is not often that an older, established artist will speak in such glowing and unenvious terms of a gifted younger colleague, but this was a special case—Haydn's generosity was proverbial, and Mozart's abilities struck him as miraculous. Once, when someone asked him to write a comic opera, Haydn suggested that Mozart be commissioned instead—indeed, he wanted to im-

press every patron of music with his own judgment of "how inimitable are Mozart's works, how profound, how musically intelligent, how extraordinarily sensitive!"

But Mozart's role in Viennese musical life was very different from Haydn's. He was not a "princely *Kapellmeister*," dressed in a splendid livery of light blue with silver trimmings, but a free-lance artist without a permanent employer, dependent on the vicissitudes of the music market at a time when copyright laws and performance royalties were still undreamed-of. In 1781, when he moved to Vienna from his native Salzburg, Mozart was no longer a child prodigy but a young man of twenty-five hoping to earn a living as a pianist. As he wrote to his father shortly after his arrival, "The Viennese are a people who don't mind shooting down newcomers, but only at the theatre: my métier is so well liked here that I will have no difficulty supporting myself. This is certainly the country of claviers!"

Yet in spite of the fact that he was the greatest keyboard virtuoso of his time, it was not easy to support himself and his young wife, Constanze, by playing the piano. At the ballroom called *Mehlgrube* on the Neuer Markt, where he gave a series of concerts, all the other participants, except the wind players, were amateur musicians, and the adjoining rooms offered gambling and refreshments in order to attract an audience. He also played at the Augarten, then a vast park with a restaurant at one end (now the home of the Austrian national porcelain factory). A young impresario, Philipp Jakob

Martin, had obtained a charter from the emperor entitling him to stage twelve concerts at the Augarten restaurant and four serenade-concerts in the city's most important squares; subscriptions for the entire series were to cost two ducats per person (about $20 in today's terms). Mozart's letters in the spring of 1782 are full of reports on his preparations for this subscription series:

> Tomorrow is our first *Musick* in the Augarten. At half past eight Martin is coming with a carriage. Then we have six visits to make. I must be finished with these at eleven o'clock because I must go to see Countess Rumbeck [one of the sponsors]. Then I am dining with Countess Thun [another influential patroness], in her garden, be it noted. In the evening we will rehearse the *Musique.* A symphony by Baron van Swieten and one of mine are being played. An amateur named Mademoiselle Berger is going to sing; a boy named Türk will play a violin concerto, and Fräulein von Auernhammer and I will play my E flat concerto for two pianos.

Under such circumstances, concert life in Vienna was an unpredictable and largely unprofitable affair—and although Mozart was pleased at the large number of prominent music lovers who had attended his performances, the financial returns failed to meet his expectations. As a musician without a salaried post, he was wholly dependent on the goodwill and largesse of the Viennese aristocracy, a distinguished and appreciative class, though most of its members were notoriously tight-fisted when

it came to "invisibles" like music. The upshot was that he gave piano lessons for a living, and wrote music on commission for special occasions. The court opera seemed to present the likeliest opportunities for success, but for a long time he was unable to find a libretto that suited his talents. It was clear to him that he needed to find a poet: "The best thing of all," he told his father, "is when a good composer, who understands the stage and is talented enough to make sound suggestions, meets an able poet, that true phoenix. . . ."

In the absence of an operatic success, there were other fields to conquer. Mozart loved to dance—"his body was perpetually in motion," reported his first biographer, Friedrich von Schlichtegroll; "he was either playing with his hands or beating the ground with his foot." One way to satisfy his kinetic instincts was to write dance music for the vast Redoutensaal in the Hofburg, where the great costume balls were held at Carnival time. "The people of Vienna were in my time dancing mad," reports the Irish tenor Michael Kelly, who lived in the city during the 1780s and became a close friend of Mozart's. "As the Carnival approached, gaiety began to display itself on all sides, and when it really came, nothing could exceed its brilliancy":

The ridotto rooms [Redoutensaal], where the masquerades took place, were in the palace, and spacious and commodious as they were, they were actually crammed with masqueraders. I never saw, or indeed heard of any suite of rooms, where elegance and convenience were more considered; for

the propensity of the Vienna ladies for dancing and going to carnival masquerades was so determined, that nothing was permitted to interfere with their enjoyment of their favorite amusement—nay, so notorious was it, that, for the sake of ladies in the family way, who could not be persuaded to stay at home, there were apartments prepared, with every convenience, for their accouchement, should they be unfortunately required. . . . The ladies of Vienna are particularly celebrated for their grace and movements in waltzing, of which they never tire. For my own part, I thought waltzing from ten at night until seven in the morning, a continual whirligig.

During the Carnival of 1786, Mozart himself, disguised as a "Hindu philosopher," passed out pamphlets with riddles and maxims of his own devising: among other things, they poked fun at the aristocratic numbskulls whose snobbism he found so intolerable during the rest of the social season. But this was also the year in which he began his memorable collaboration with Lorenzo da Ponte and produced the first of the three operas which were to revolutionize the musical theater. Da Ponte was a poet disguised as an abbé, a baptized Jew from Venice—an accomplished libertine, humorist, humanist, court playwright to the emperor Joseph II, and probably the finest opera librettist ever to set pen to paper. For the first and last time in his life, Mozart worked with texts that were worthy of his music—*Le Nozze di Figaro* (*The Marriage of Figaro*) in 1786, *Don Giovanni* a year later, and *Così fan*

Below: This room in a typically Viennese townhouse near St. Stephen's Cathedral is where Mozart composed The Marriage of Figaro *and played quartets with Haydn and his friends. It is also where, in 1787, on a short visit to Vienna, the seventeen-year-old Beethoven sought him out. Left: Mozart's copybook, open to a page of his unfinished* Requiem, *on which he was working at the time of his death in 1791.*

tutte (*Women Are Like That*) in 1789. The first of these is adapted from *Le mariage de Figaro* by Pierre de Beaumarchais, an utterly subversive French play that had been banned from the imperial stages but was now smuggled into the opera house by the back door—slightly expurgated, but all the more powerful and delightful as a piece of anti-authoritarian theater. *Figaro* made a name for Mozart and da Ponte not only in Vienna but also in Prague, where it created an instant sensation. "Here they talk about nothing but *Figaro*," Mozart was happy to report. "Nothing is played, sung or whistled but *Figaro*. No opera is drawing like *Figaro*. Nothing, nothing but *Figaro*."

Riding the crest of this enthusiasm, the composer and librettist were then commissioned to write a new work for the Prague Opera, which they did in Vienna during the summer of 1787. Mozart seems to have had no inkling that they had created a work which, like *Hamlet,* would remain an object of perpetual fascination to people both in and out of the theater, a source of continuing joy and wonderment to the best brains of Western civilization. Since its first performance, *Don Giovanni* (or *The Stone Guest*) has been an aesthetic beacon that always illuminates some new aspect of the intellectual landscape, serving musicians as a constant "classicall" point of reference and providing literati with endless grist for their mill. The poet E. T. A. Hoffmann dated the beginning of the Romantic movement from this music. The philosopher Søren Kierkegaard looked upon it as the quintessence of human life.

Early in the twentieth century the Viennese psychoanalyst Otto Rank described the opera as the most inspired form of the archetypal Oedipus drama. His extraordinary essay, *Die Don-Juan Gestalt,* interprets the "Stone Guest" in the opera's cemetery scene as the vengeful spirit of the murdered primal father, the Don's comic servant Leporello as the voice of his master's guilty conscience, and the Don himself as the liberated Oedipus who has come to terms with his psyche: "The overwhelming greatness of the Don Juan *Gestalt* lies in the fact that he has shed the heroic lie. . . ."

Mozart and da Ponte, of course, thought they were merely bringing new ideas to the rather worn-out stereotypes of the Italian opera. Their third masterpiece was no less audacious, yet for a long time it was overshadowed by the other two. "It was too much even for the cultivated Viennese to understand," writes the American musicologist H. C. Robbins Landon, who has made a lifetime study of the Viennese classical period; "indeed it has taken 150 years for *Così fan tutte* to be recognized as the supreme music drama that it is."

Mozart applied his experience with Italian opera to one notable German opera, *Die Zauberflöte* (*The Magic Flute*), but it suffers from a patchwork libretto which is redeemed only by some of Mozart's finest music. Unfortunately, even his triumphs at the opera house were insufficient to solve his ongoing financial dilemma. Though Joseph II did finally appoint him "composer to the imperial court"—800 gulden per annum for writing the dance music for the Redoutensaal—he was repeatedly forced to ap-

Above left: The first few measures of Mozart's autograph score of his Piano Sonata in A minor (K. 310). The manuscript is signed and dated 1778—written the summer he was in Paris with his mother, who died there less than four months after their arrival. Above: An unfinished portrait of Mozart at the keyboard, painted by Joseph Lange in the winter of 1782-83. The composer had married Costanze Weber the summer before, and the next few years were to be the happiest of his adult life, with the widening acceptance of his music in the city. From this time date many of the piano concertos wherein the solo instrument interracts with the orchestra in an unprecedented way, foreshadowing Beethoven's concertos.

When Mozart died on December 5, 1791, **The Magic Flute** *was playing to full houses at the Freihaus Theatre—but from the records of St. Stephen's parish it is known that barely enough money was paid by his grief-stricken wife Constanze for a third-class funeral. Wolfgang Amadeus, "Beloved of God," was buried outside the city walls in a grave shared with several others. There was no gravestone, and the composer's remains have never been found. Although his music was never forgotten, either by fastidious connoisseurs or by countless common people who recalled his melodies, it was not until many years later that this touching memorial was erected to his memory.*

peal to his friends for charity disguised as loans. The trajectory of his life had been moving steadily upward, fulfilling the promise of his youth as the most gifted of child prodigies; then suddenly it took a sharp downward turn and was cut short at the age of thirty-five. He was at work on his great, unfinished *Requiem* almost until the day of his death; it had been commissioned by an Austrian count who intended to pass it off as a work of his own composition. (Only Mozart's untimely demise prevented the count from carrying out this ignoble enterprise.) It was the final irony in a life full of paradoxes; indeed, Mozart had prophesied, when he accepted the assignment, that he was writing this *Requiem* for himself.

Franz Joseph Haydn always broke into tears, afterward, whenever Mozart's sons came to visit him. He had been in London when he heard the news of Mozart's death, and had written to Frau von Genzinger that "Posterity will not see such a talent again in 100 years!" He himself lived to the age of seventy-seven, retiring to a small house in the Viennese suburb of Gumpendorf which became a place of pilgrimage for music lovers from all over the world. The city honored him repeatedly as the great elder statesman of Austrian music, the hero of an age that was fast drawing to a close.

His death, in fact, coincided exactly with a traumatic event in Viennese history—the bombardment and occupation of the city by Napoleon's forces in 1809. During the cannonade, French artillery came within yards of hitting Haydn's house, and though the aged composer assured his servants that

no harm would come to them, the shock proved too much for his system: Haydn took to his bed and died three weeks later. Stendhal, "the first modern man" (who was to French literature what Mozart was to Austrian music), arrived with the French army as one of Napoleon's quartermasters and was just in time to attend the state *Requiem* mass at which both French and Austrian officials paid tribute to Haydn's memory. "I saw there some generals and administrators of the French army, who appeared affected with the loss which the arts had just sustained," Stendhal later recalled. Attending Haydn's *Requiem* gave him the idea of writing his first book, a largely plagiarized biography of Haydn, Mozart, and Metastasio.

The new, Napoleonic "romantics" were bidding farewell to the "classicists" and their age. In contrast to their impetuous drive toward emotional self-expression, there had always been a sense of containment and of devotion to a higher purpose in Haydn's music. As he had explained to a group of his admirers a few years before his death, "Often when I was struggling against obstacles of all kinds, often when strength of mind and body failed me and it was difficult for me to persevere in the course upon which I had set out, a secret feeling whispered to me: 'There are so few happy and contented people here below, everywhere men are oppressed by trouble and care; perhaps your labor may sometimes be a source from which those who are burdened with care may derive a moment's respite and refreshment.' Here was a powerful incentive for carrying on."

The bombardment of Vienna depicted in this old painting can be identified as artillery action following the battle of Wagram (1809), when Napoleon Bonaparte invested the city with the largest concentration of cannon fire hitherto massed. The skyline includes the easily recognizable spire of St. Stephen's, the smaller steeple of the Michaelerkirche to its right, and the barely visible dome of the Karlskirche to its left—indicating that the scene is viewed from a height north of the city, probably the Kahlenberg. Napoleon himself is standing in the small group of figures at center foreground. To his left and right are members of emperor's grenadier guards, easily recognizable by their uniforms. The fact that Napoleon was able to take Vienna without breaching its medieval fortifications was cited, fifty years later, as the main argument for their demolition, making way for the great Ringstrasse urban development.

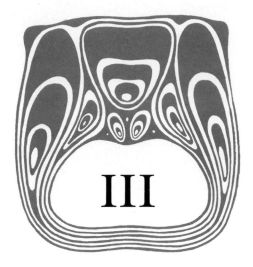

III

The bombardment of Vienna that hastened Haydn's death was symptomatic of the political storms that were sweeping across Europe. The fall of the Bastille, the proclamation of the French republic, Napoleon's rise to power and his conquests in Italy and Germany had created a whole series of new political realities and expectations. The old legitimist systems seemed incapable of withstanding the onslaughts of Napoleon's battalions, representing the new ideas and efficiencies of a nation ruled by self-made men. Napoleon, the ex-artillery officer who had crowned himself emperor, had bested the hereditary rulers of Europe at every turn.

The Habsburgs tried to reverse the tide and suffered a series of defeats—until the emperor Francis I resolved the crisis by resorting to the marrying tactics of his ancestors. He sealed an alliance with the parvenu monarch by sending his daughter, Marie Louise, to become Napoleon's duly-wedded empress. For a few years, at least, the harmony of Europe seemed to be restored.

The Viennese watched these maneuvers at the summit level and found it difficult to repress their disloyal and seditious thoughts. If a Corsican upstart could win the hand of a Habsburg princess, anything was possible—perhaps even government by the people. There were times, especially at the beginning of the short-lived French experiment with democracy, when many Viennese intellectuals thought longingly of an Austrian republic. But the first stirrings of unrest were promptly suppressed by the police. "Here they have been arresting several persons of importance," reported the young

Beethoven to his publisher, Nikolaus Simrock, in 1794. He was still a newcomer to the city, but he had seen enough of Vienna to understand its essential character. "They say a revolution was about to break out—but I believe that as long as the Austrians have brown beer and sausages, they'll never revolt."

Like virtually all the artists and intellectuals of his generation, Beethoven looked on General Bonaparte, at first, as the personification of the spirit with which the new century confronted the old—youth, energy, courage, ambition. This brilliant tactician seemed to be the shining example of the self-made man who owed his meteoric rise to his own abilities rather than the privileges of birth. Indeed, Beethoven wrote his most "revolutionary" symphony, the *Eroica,* "with Bonaparte in mind"; that is, its heroic, declamatory music was intended as a tribute to Bonaparte the First Consul, who represented the republican principles that Beethoven admired. All the more bitter was his subsequent disillusionment. He had already sent a copy of the score to Paris through the French embassy in Vienna, early in 1804. Later that year, however, the thirty-four-year-old Napoleon was proclaimed emperor of the French, and Beethoven became infuriated when his friend Ferdinand Ries brought him the news. As Ries reports, "He flew into a rage and cried out, 'Then he, too, is just an ordinary man? Now he will trample underfoot all the Rights of Man and only indulge his ambition!'" He seized a copy of the score of his new symphony and tore up the title page with its dedication, "written in

The Congress Dances

honor of Bonaparte." It was replaced with the non-committal title, *Sinfonia eroica,* and an allusive sub-title: "To celebrate the memory of a great man." Actually, it was to celebrate a great ideal that Beethoven had written this passionate symphony—the same democratic ideal of brotherhood that dominates the last movement of his Ninth Symphony.

It was characteristic of the times—and of Vienna—that despite its revolutionary sentiments, the *Eroica* was given its first performance by a private orchestra in the palace of Prince Lobkowitz, one of the richest nobles and one of the foremost music lovers of the city. Soon afterward, in fact, the prince had it performed a second time at his country palace, this time for Prince Louis Ferdinand of Prussia, a musical enthusiast (soon to be killed fighting against Napoleon) who liked the work so much that he asked for the whole symphony to be repeated as an encore.

As we have seen, Beethoven's position in the marble music rooms of the Viennese aristocracy was very different from that of Haydn, or even Mozart. Far from being content to lead the life of a court composer, Beethoven insisted on his prerogatives as a creative artist. A generation of *Sturm und Drang* in literature and philosophy had prepared the cultivated public for the idea that the creative musician was no longer an entertainer or a sort of functionary; he was the creator of the highest values of human civilization. In 1805, when his friend and patron Prince Lichnowsky inadvertently injured Beethoven's pride (something that was very easy to do), he received a short lecture on the subject

of manners and prerogatives that put him firmly in his place: "Prince! What you are you are by circumstance and by birth. What I am, I am through myself. Of princes there have been and will be thousands. Of Beethovens there is only one."

The Viennese who cared about serious music were wholly in agreement. Even the Archduke Rudolf, youngest half-brother of the emperor Franz, was quite prepared to waive the rules of court protocol in order to remain on good terms with Beethoven, who had agreed to give him piano lessons. Beethoven, from the first, had no compunctions about rapping the archduke's imperial knuckles when he made mistakes, and he stated in no uncertain terms that he could not be bothered to observe the niceties of court ceremonial. Unperturbed, Rudolf "gave directions that Beethoven should be allowed to go his own way undisturbed. It was his nature and could not be altered."

The Beethoven years were the Viennese aristocracy's finest era. No longer certain of their inherited prerogatives, they sensed that what was most worth preserving in that uneasy epoch was the music of this abrasive, ill-humored composer whose temper was not improved by the fact that he was going deaf. They were not wrong in their judgment. In some indefinable way, Beethoven's music established a new standard of excellence in human affairs. Its passionate eloquence begins where words fail—intensely serious, tragic, and demanding of the utmost concentration. Keats's line, "There is a budding morrow in midnight," suggests something of the mingled hope and sorrow that find joint ex-

pression in Beethoven's sonatas and string quartets. Hector Berlioz was to call them "the extra-human meditations of the *génie panthéiste.*" It was no wonder that his listeners were moved to tears when they first heard this music. "It is so expressive one cannot play it," said the Baroness von Ertmann about the slow movement of the trio he wrote for her but dedicated to Rudolf, the so-called *Archduke Trio.* Nearly two hundred years later, musicians still speak in the same hushed tones about "late Beethoven"— the great touchstone and enigma of chamber music. In his own day, only the most dedicated of his admirers could follow his intentions, and the more conventional musicians were profoundly puzzled by his dissonances. "You surely do not consider these works to be *music?*" he was asked by an impertinent violinist, Felix Radicati, who was helping him with the fingering of the Opus 59 quartets. "Oh, they are not for you," was Beethoven's answer, "but for a later age!"

But the real music lovers of Vienna knew perfectly well what they had in this man. Only once during his thirty-five years in the city were they in danger of losing him—when Napoleon's brother, King Jerome of Westphalia, offered him a well-paid post as court *Kapellmeister* in 1809. To keep their star composer in Vienna, three leading patrons of music made a counteroffer: they would provide a lifetime annuity of 4,000 florins (today about $30,000) "to put Herr Ludwig van Beethoven in a position where material needs shall cause him no inconvenience or inhibit his powerful genius." The three guarantors were Archduke Rudolf, Prince Lobkowitz,

and Prince Kinsky; their contract with Beethoven explicitly states that the composer "binds himself to reside in Vienna. . . ."

Musical conditions in Beethoven's Vienna also left something to be desired. As yet there was no professional symphony orchestra to play his music—the Vienna Philharmonic was not founded until 1842 and did not really begin to function until 1854. Instead he had recourse to amateur groups, the *Liebhaber* ("Music Lover") and the *Musikfreunde* ("Friends of Music") associations, consisting of thirty or forty non-professional string players, reinforced by professional wind players and first-desk men. These groups rarely held rehearsals—it was not a sporting thing for gentlemen to do, and besides the pleasure was in the playing, not the listening; admission was by invitation only.

To bring his works before a larger public, Beethoven would organize "musical academies" (i.e., concerts) for which he would hire one of the city's theater orchestras and add other likely players, amateur or professional, much as modern recordings are often made by "pickup groups." Unfortunately they were often hastily rehearsed, haphazardly manned, and psychologically unprepared for performing this difficult and unconventional music. Though the musicians usually complained that his symphonies were "impossible" to play, he rarely had more than two or three rehearsals at which to achieve some semblance of unity and phrasing.

For the first performance of the Fifth and Sixth symphonies, for example, Beethoven found it impossible to obtain a single full rehearsal for all the

The modern Viennese artist Wilhelm Thöny's graphic evocation of Beethoven at the piano (far left) recalls the electrifying effect the composer had on his listeners (left). Beethoven dedicated three piano sonatas (right), published in 1796, as homage to Franz Joseph Haydn. Haydn's esteem was no less valuable to Beethoven than the patronage of that music-loving prince, Franz Joseph Lobkowitz, in whose palace (below) many of his compositions were first played. Beethoven dedicated important works, including the Eroica, to Lobkowitz.

TROIS · SONATES
Pour le Clavecin ou Piano-Forte
Composées et Dédiées
A Mr. Joseph Haydn
Maître de Chapelle de S. A. Monseigneur le Prince Esterhazy &c.
par
LOUIS van BEETHOVEN
Oeuvre II.
A Vienne chez Artaria et Compe.

works to be performed, though each contained formidable problems. The program was to last four full hours and contained, besides the symphonies, parts of his C Major Mass, the aria *Ah! Perfido!*, a piano concerto (probably the Fourth), an improvisation for piano solo, and a major work for piano, orchestra, and chorus, the *Choral Fantasy*—all of them "completely new and not yet heard in public," as the announcements pointed out. The date was December 22, 1808, and it was bitter cold in the unheated Theater an der Wien. The audience sat in the boxes wrapped in furs and winter coats; the musicians shivered onstage. During the last work, the *Choral Fantasy,* the exhausted players finally gave way under the strain. "The clarinets make a mistake in the count and enter too soon," noted one musical reporter. "A curious mixture of tones results, Beethoven jumps up, tries to silence the clarinets, but does not succeed until he has called out quite loudly and rather ill-temperedly: 'Stop, stop! That won't do! Again—again!'"

He was hard of hearing by then, and this was his last public appearance as a piano soloist. After this unhappy experience he preferred to let other pianists perform his concertos. But he persisted in conducting the premières of his new symphonies. He introduced the Seventh and Eighth symphonies at a private audition for Archduke Rudolf and his friends in April 1813, with a very modest orchestra: "For the symphonies I should like to have at least four first violins, four violas, two basses and two cellos." Later he gave a public performance of the Seventh with a heavily reinforced orchestra. Again

The highly successful theatrical producer Emanuel Schikaneder, who had made a fortune on Mozart's The Magic Flute, was the first licensee of the renowned Theater-an-der-Wien (right) when it opened in 1801. The sculptural group over the Neoclassical portal commemorates Schikaneder as Papageno in The Magic Flute, with his bird cage and feathered amoretti. With an eye to future productions, Schikaneder gave Beethoven a year's free lodging in the theater and engaged him to compose the music for the opera Fidelio, which was a complete failure on its first performance there in November 1805. After the text had been recast, Fidelio enjoyed a resounding success in May 1814. Beethoven had become a revered public figure and, in contrast to Mozart, his death on March 26, 1827, was the occasion for universal mourning. The oil sketch of Beethoven's hands (left) by J. Danhauser, painted two days after his death, is a manifestation of music's loss.

there was trouble during the rehearsals; as one witness noted, "the violinists absolutely refused to play one episode in the symphony, and reproached him for writing passages that are impossible to execute." With more tact than usual he cajoled them into studying the parts on their own time. "If you practice it at home the music will surely go," he suggested, and it did. The result was a performance that the *cognoscenti* described as "wholly masterful," though Beethoven's conducting—he could hear only the loudest tones of the orchestra—struck many onlookers as ridiculous and pathetic.

He had, by this time, built up a very large store of resentment against the bulk of the Viennese musical public. People who went to visit him came away with reports of Beethoven denouncing the frivolity of local audiences. "From the emperor to the boot-black," he liked to say, "all the Viennese are worthless." He would deliver great diatribes on the subject: "From top to bottom everyone is a scoundrel. One can trust no one." Besides, they had no real taste in music. "The Viennese, he can only talk about eating and drinking, and sings and strums music of little significance," he declared. "No one has any understanding now for what is good and strong, for true music, in fact! Yes, that's how it is, you Viennese!"

Beethoven had good reason to complain about the mediocrity of Viennese popular music. While he himself was at work at some of the most complex and cerebral music ever written, the average music lover was strumming the guitar and singing what Beethoven considered "soulless" ditties—"miser-

able bunglings, which you use to ruin yourselves for true art"—for which there was a profitable market and an enthusiastic audience.

There was little common ground between the guitar strummers and the Beethoven connoisseurs, the parlor ditties and the monumental string quartets. And yet the average Viennese spoke in respectful and admiring terms of this lonely and eccentric figure whom the press described as "our famous tonesetter, Beethoven." He was not, as is sometimes suggested, a neglected genius living in poverty and obscurity; to his fellow citizens he was "*Der* Beethoven"—a living legend and a celebrity, renowned for his personal quirks as well as for his music, which was played by serious musicians throughout Europe.

Even so, Europe went on beating a path to his door. He reached the height of his fame just as Vienna itself became the focal point of post-Napoleonic politics. Napoleon's defeat and abdication, following the destruction of his armies in Russia and Spain, had created the need for a new system of European relationships, an international order that would provide the basis for a lasting peace. To that end, the victorious allies—Austria, Russia, Prussia, and Great Britain—convoked the Congress of Vienna in October 1814, to decide the fate of all the territories that had been conquered by the French and were now to be returned to their rightful owners—or placed in more deserving hands. "Our business," declared the emperor Francis I of Austria, "is to give the world that repose which Napoleon has troubled all these years."

Under the skillful guidance of the young Austrian foreign minister, Prince Metternich, the Congress did manage to establish the all-important balance of power among the major nations which prevented another full-scale European war until 1870. The Congress lasted for five months, and more than 100,000 visitors flocked to Vienna for the occasion. It was like a giant party at which the victors could celebrate Napoleon's downfall. Though the Austrian court had been impoverished by the wars, the city provided the ideal meeting-ground (psychologically as well as geographically) for the monarchs of Europe and their principal ministers: Czar Alexander of Russia; Lord Castlereagh, the British foreign secretary; Prince Talleyrand, representing the interests of a France now ruled by the aging Louis XVIII; the king of Prussia, Friedrich Wilhelm II, and the deft, elegant Metternich. All told there were 247 members of reigning houses (which created untold problems of protocol until the young czar suggested that kings be ranked by precedence of birth-date), together with their staffs and retainers—generals, diplomats, nobles, lawyers, financiers, journalists, cartographers, as well as wives, mistresses, and fortune-hunting ladies of every nationality.

They spent those five months bargaining over the fate of whole nations—Italy, Switzerland, the Low Countries, Saxony, Poland—making decisions that have come back to haunt the peoples of Europe. But the Congress also had its social and cultural side. There were endless balls and banquets, gala performances in the theaters and concert halls,

hunting parties, a balloon ascent from the Augarten, and *tableaux vivants* in which lovely, titled young ladies gave representations of "Hippolytus Defending His Virtue Before Theseus" and other stirring moments from classical mythology.

Beethoven's *Fidelio*, with its great theme of liberation, became the opera of the hour when it was specially revived for the Congress. It had been a failure in previous productions, but now, with a revised score and a new overture, it was "received with tempestuous applause." The Seventh Symphony was also repeated, together with the *Battle Symphony* and another crowd-pleaser, a cantata for solo voices, chorus, and orchestra especially composed for the occasion, entitled *Der glorreiche Augenblick* ("The Glorious Moment"). For Beethoven and his librettist, Alois Weissenbach, it was this very Congress of Vienna that marked a "glorious moment" in the history of the world. The concert at which they gave the first performance of the cantata took place in the Redoutensaal on November 29, 1814, and was attended by scores of notables, including the empress of Austria, the czar and czarina of Russia, and the king of Prussia.

The wars had been made in Paris; the peace was being forged in Vienna. "You have come at the proper time to behold great events," the elderly Prince de Ligne told the young noblemen at the Congress. "Europe is in Vienna. The web of politics is shot through with festivities." The emperor's palaces became the scene of extraordinary ceremonials and the honorific bestowing of gifts from one monarch to another. The coveted British Order of the

Garter was bestowed on the emperor of Austria, and soon every other nation followed suit with orders, crosses, and decorations. When there were no more honors to pass out, some of the monarchs who were present began to give one another regiments in their armies. The emperor of Austria presented his "Hiller" Regiment to the czar, and Alexander reciprocated by giving Franz a regiment of his Imperial Guard.

Some of the people whose careers had depended on Napoleon's patronage were able to recoup their losses by putting in a timely appearance at the Congress. A typical case was that of Jean-Baptiste Isabey, a portrait painter who had risen to prominence at Napoleon's court and had lost all his best clients after the emperor's exile. Talleyrand advised him to seek his fortune in Vienna, where he was able to make a dramatic comeback by setting up a portrait studio in Leopoldstadt, where he painted an endless succession of rulers and princes. "Isabey lived in splendor, as once Benvenuto Cellini had in the Louvre," noted the Count de La Garde. "The walls of his atelier were entirely covered with sketches of his paintings and outlines of his paintings; it resembled a magic lantern in which could be seen, one after another, all the personages of the Congress."

It was Isabey who painted the famous group portrait of the leaders of the Congress that is reproduced in all the history books—twenty-three of the most powerful men in Europe, sitting or standing around the conference table on which they redrew the map of the continent. It was an enterprise of great pith and moment—but it has also been called "mainly a scramble for territory and power."

The allied leaders had counted, however, without the energy and resourcefulness of the man they had exiled to Elba. At six o'clock on the morning of March 7, 1815, Metternich's valet brought a dispatch to his bedside announcing Napoleon's escape from the island. Four hours later, after a meeting of the rulers of Russia, Austria, and Prussia, war was declared and "aides-de-camp were flying in all directions carrying to the several army corps, who were retiring, the order to halt." When the Congress learned that Napoleon had reentered Paris and again made himself master of France, "a thousand candles seemed in a single instant to have been extinguished," as the Count de La Garde noted. Yet the assembled diplomats soon regained their nerve and momentum. The Duke of Wellington was dispatched to the Low Countries to deal with Napoleon, and the non-military delegates continued to draw their maps of the postwar world. In fact, the final act of the Congress was signed on June 9, 1815; eleven days later Napoleon was crushed at Waterloo.

The Congress of Vienna thus marked a watershed in modern history. It also, incidentally, established the Viennese waltz as the reigning ballroom dance of nineteenth-century Europe. For a dozen years or more the waltz had been edging its merry way into polite society, creating a furor at every turn. It was the modern version of a medieval turning dance that had, from the very beginning, drawn the fire of clerics and guardians of public decency.

Metternich conceived of the Congress of Vienna not merely as a gathering of representatives from all the powers for a political transformation of Europe, but also as a great Peace Festival to mark the beginning of a new era. Day after day, night after night, there were receptions, balls, theatricals, and military exercises. One of the most resplendent occasions was the bal paré *(evening-dress ball) given by the emperor and empress on October 9, 1814, in the Winter Riding School, recorded in this watercolor by the contemporary artist Johann Nepomuk Hochle. The women wore dresses of white, pale blue, or rose; the men were in uniform or dressed in blue or black tailcoats with white or blue breeches; and all blazed with jewels. In the intermezzo, twenty-four of the most beautiful women of the court, costumed as the Four Elements, gave an allegorical tableau vivant for the assembled guests.*

A dance in which men put their arms around women and whirled around the floor was nothing but "a wild, appallingly bestial rushing, running and whirling round one another," and pious young men were warned to refrain from contact with "those damsels who are fond of night-dances and love to be whirled round and kissed indecently and allow themselves to be touched and handled."

Somehow, the Viennese managed to survive these hazards, and to make *walzen* (literally, "revolving") their favorite pastime. "Few women, only those with iron characters, are indifferent to its entrancing swing," reported the *Journal des Luxus und der Moden* in 1797. "Most of them are most reluctant to obey their mothers and to give up this Bacchanalian revel in order to safeguard their health." The authorities in neighboring Germany and Switzerland prohibited waltzing in a vain attempt to prevent its spread.

In the end, no considerations of health or moral welfare could impede the triumphal onward whirl of the Viennese waltz. The first of the city's great waltz emporia, the *Mondscheinsaal* ("Moonlight Hall"), acquired the reputation of having caused innumerable casualties among the young men who frequented it. "It was *bon ton* to be a virtuoso dancer, to waltz with one's partner from one corner of the hall to the opposite corner in the most rapid tempo," recalled Adolf Bäuerle. The full circle had to be done six or eight times, breathlessly and without a pause, as each couple tried to outshine the other. "Not seldom did this frenzy end for one of the parties in an apoplexy of the lungs."

Soon the first waltz-halls were dwarfed by the

spacious *Sperl,* opened in 1807, and the enormous *Apollo Palace,* inaugurated a year later. The latter contained five large and thirty-one smaller ballrooms in which 6,000 people could dance the evening away. For the next few years the *Apollo* served as the very heart of the Viennese amusement world. When the Congress assembled in Vienna, the rest of Europe learned to waltz in the Viennese fashion—though when dances were held at court, this exciting novelty continued to coexist, for a time, with the minuet of the *ancien régime.* One of the things virtually all the foreign delegates took away from Vienna was the art of moving their feet in the various patterns of the waltz—the slow waltz, the *sauteuse* waltz, and the *jetté* or quick *sauteuse* waltz, each with its special steps. Indeed, the delegates did so much dancing that critics coined the famous epigram, *"Le congrès danse, mais il ne marche pas":* "the Congress dances, but it doesn't move"—i.e., no work gets done. Yet it was evident that dancing and diplomacy could go hand in hand, and when the maps were drawn and the ball was over, even the staid and proper British could not refrain from taking the waltz home with them. A year later, in 1816, a London dancing master, Th. Wilson, published the first English book on the subject, *A description of the correct method of waltzing,* in which he refuted once and for all the terrible charge that waltzing was an enemy of morals and a danger to virtue.

Beethoven, meanwhile, though usually concerned with weightier matters, had not ignored the century's headlong rush into three-quarter time. His piano music frequently borrows from the waltz and its country cousin, the *Ländler.* And he composed one of his most stupendous sets of variations on a simple Viennese waltz tune. A local publisher, Anton Diabelli, had composed a short, catchy waltz which he sent to several composers with the suggestion that they write a collective set of variations on it. Beethoven declined to join the others, but then decided that this mere "cobbler's patch" *(Schusterfleck)* of a tune could be made the basis of a fully developed set of variations. He did not stop, in fact, until he had produced the monumental set of thirty-three variations, Opus 120, which Diabelli correctly announced in the *Wiener Zeitung* of June 16, 1823, as "a great and important masterpiece. . . . as only Beethoven, the greatest living representative of true art, can produce."

The greatest early master of the Viennese waltz, however, was not Beethoven but Franz Schubert, the young composer who lived all of his thirty-one years in Beethoven's shadow. Schubert belonged to a younger generation—he was twenty-seven years Beethoven's junior—and it was people his age, the young students, artists, and professional musicians, who made the waltz a Viennese institution. As his friend Leopold von Sonnleithner recalled, Schubert would often play at the private balls of families with which he was acquainted: "He never danced but he was always ready to sit down at the piano, where for hours he improvised the most beautiful waltzes; those he liked he repeated in order to remember them and write them out afterwards."

The simple pleasures of Biedermeier life are reflected in this painting by Leopold Kupelwieser, an intimate and lifelong friend of Franz Schubert. Seated at left with his hand resting on a small piano, Schubert watches a charade of The Expulsion of Adam and Eve from Paradise enacted by a group of young men and women. The occasion was a holiday gathering in the summer of 1820 in a small castle at Atzenbrugg, a few miles from Vienna. Schubert was so fond of Kupelwieser that he insisted on playing dance music for his friend's wedding a few years later. An improvised waltz tune so charmed the bride that she never forgot it; it was passed on to her children and grandchildren, never recorded and only preserved by ear for over a hundred years.

Schubert was poor and almost unknown; he moved in far less rarefied circles than those for which Beethoven had played. For that very reason he was more closely in touch with the popular music of his time, especially the waltzes, *Ländler,* and songs that he played to perfection for his friends. Yet he was no less serious in his approach to music than his two idols, Mozart and Beethoven. While most of the other Viennese composers of his generation were turning out potboilers that have long since been forgotten, Schubert created music of extraordinary poetry and beauty—the *Trout* Quintet, for example, and the *Wanderer* Fantasy. "After Beethoven, who can do anything more?" he used to ask, yet he found ways of doing something more by pursuing his own intensely lyrical course. Beethoven's formidable presence always intimidated Schubert, and though he had often seen Bethoven in concerts and at restaurants, and they had many friends in common, he was not actually introduced to Beethoven until the older composer was already on his deathbed, in 1827. Beethoven had only recently become acquainted with a large collection of Schubert's songs; according to his factotum, Anton Schindler, "he was astonished at their number and could not be made to believe that Schubert had by then written more than five hundred."

When Beethoven, a week before his death, heard that Schubert and another friend had come to pay their respects, he told Schindler, "Let Schubert come in first." But nothing else is known about the only meeting of these two extraordinary composers who made the first third of the nineteenth century an era of unrivaled greatness in the musical history of Vienna and the Western world.

The Schubert songs that excited Beethoven's belated admiration are the perfect expression, in music, of that elusive and delightful style known as Biedermeier. In place of the massive grandeur of an *Eroica,* there is the refined and melancholy lyricism of *An die Musik, Der Lindenbaum,* and *Death and the Maiden.* Though the Biedermeier style was an offspring of Romanticism, it was the gentle daughter of a stormy and impassioned age; a romanticism that has turned inward and concerns itself with the quiet joys of domestic life. Instead of painting battle scenes or the deaths of Roman heroes, Biedermeier artists preferred to depict pretty girls gazing wistfully out of the windows of their drawing-rooms; like sundials, they recorded only the brightest moments of the age.

The term Biedermeier requires some explanation, for even in German it is a very elastic concept. It is now applied to a whole epoch of the German and Austrian arts—roughly from 1814 to 1860; that is, beginning with the Congress of Vienna and reaching fruition by 1848, the year of the pan-European revolution. Biedermeier furniture, which has become very famous and immensely valuable, was essentially that made for the comfortable middle classes, a softened and simplified version of the more ambitious, rigorous Empire style. One sits far more comfortably in Biedermeier armchairs and chaises-longues than on Empire chairs and sofas. The term itself was coined in the 1850s by two Heidelberg poets, Adolf Kussmaul and Ludwig

Eichrodt, who had discovered the collected verse of an obscure Swabian schoolmaster and then proceeded to write a whole series of parody-poems in the same naïve vein. The fictitious author of these rustic verses was "Gottlieb Biedermaier" (with an *a*), a name that had overtones of old-fashioned, god-fearing simplicity, for *bieder* means "upright," as well as "ingenuous, commonplace," and a *Meier* (or *Maier,* as the south Germans often spell it) is a tenant dairy farmer. Soon there was a *"Buch Biedermaier"* of mock-simple poems, and a whole new literary category was established. Later the term was applied retroactively to the honest, unsophisticated furniture of what, in England, would be called the Early Victorian style, and before long the whole era became known as the *Biedermeierzeit.*

The decisive quality of Biedermeier painting is its charm; like most nineteenth-century art it turns its back on the social realities of the time in order to dwell on the pleasures of simple bourgeois living. Its artists were so busy painting romantic interiors and the cobbled courtyards of half-timbered houses that they ignored the smoking factory chimneys that were beginning to loom on the horizon. This was the era of the steam engine and the milling machine, of railroads, telegraph lines, and the first mass-production methods—as well as the social and economic problems created by the industrial revolution. The Biedermeier artists saw nothing of William Blake's "dark, satanic mills," but confined themselves to pretty girls bent over their embroidery or walking among the lilac bushes.

Schubert, however, was neither an escapist nor a sentimentalist; though he ranks as the great Biedermeier composer he was profoundly observant and actively concerned with human beings and their problems. The first of his great song-cycles, *Die Schöne Müllerin* ("The Beautiful Miller's Daughter"), is in the purest, most expressive vein of Austrian Romanticism. But his last song-cycle, *Die Winterreise* ("The Winter Journey"), concludes with a grim, tragic vision of a wandering hurdy-gurdy player who symbolizes the human condition.

This was the underside of the Biedermeier coin. Thousands of traditional craftsmen had been put out of work by the steam-driven machinery of the new age, and there were beggars everywhere. They filled the courtyards and pushed their way into the churches of Vienna, where they disturbed the regular churchgoers to such an extent that the archbishop demanded a special *Religionspolizei* to deal with these unwelcome intruders. The police, however, were unable to cope with them, since the jails and poorhouses were already filled to overflowing.

For an unemployed composer like Schubert it was hardly less difficult to make a living. While he was in his twenties he had cheerfully led the life of a bohemian, supported by equally improvident friends and occasional payments from the publishers of his songs and dances. But when he began composing *Die Winterreise* in 1827, at the age of thirty, "he had become much more serious," as his friend Johann Mayerhofer recalled. "He had been long and severely ill; he had been through crushing experiences; for him life had lost its rosy hue; for him, winter had set in."

Built in 1803, the Dreimäderlhaus (left), near the northwest corner of the Inner City, is a superb example of late eighteenth-century Austrian Neoclassicism, with its rococo swags over the windows and a shell relief over the doorway. The long-standing association of this Viennese landmark with Schubert may have been prolonged by the popular 1920's operetta titled Dreimäderlhaus, *which contains adaptations of a number of Schubert melodies, including a theme from the* Unfinished Symphony *converted into a waltz tune. Only twenty months separated the deaths of Beethoven and Schubert (1827 and 1828), and they were both buried in the Währing cemetery northwest of the old city limits, Schubert having expressed a wish to be interred near Beethoven. In 1888 their remains were transferred to "tombs of honor" at the new Central Cemetery, and new gravestones were erected (right).*

He had always been in love with this city where he had been born and educated, but now he began to have second thoughts about Vienna. After a visit to Graz, in Styria, in September 1827, he wrote to a friend in terms reminiscent of Beethoven's diatribes against the Viennese: "I cannot as yet get accustomed to Vienna. True it is rather large, but then it is empty of cordiality, candor, genuine thought, reasonable words, and especially of intelligent deeds. There is so much confused chatter that one hardly knows whether one is on one's head or one's heels, and one rarely or never achieves any inward contentment." According to another of his friends, Eduard von Bauernfeld, Schubert was simply not practical enough to make a place for himself in the Viennese scheme of things.

In a sense, Schubert's career remained as unfinished as the most famous of his symphonies. He had been one of the pallbearers at Beethoven's funeral in March 1827, when 20,000 mourners filled the streets in what amounted to a state funeral for the man they called "the General of the Musicians." A year and a half later, after writing the magnificent C Major String Quintet—"the most romantically conceived work in all chamber music"—Schubert himself died of typhoid fever. There was a very quiet funeral, attended by his friends, but they laid him to rest in Währing cemetery, just one grave removed from Beethoven's. The poet Franz Grillparzer, who had written the eulogy for Beethoven, also provided the lines that were engraved on Schubert's tombstone: "Here music has entombed a rich treasure, but still fairer hopes."

IV

Prince Metternich had seen something of the mob violence of the French Revolution when he was a student in Strasbourg, and he ascribed his lifelong hatred of political innovation to this traumatic experience. The "concert of Europe" which he had composed and orchestrated so brilliantly at the Congress of Vienna was intended to prevent the recurrence of such events—particularly, to suppress the revolutionary and nationalist tendencies that were rife in the restless Habsburg-ruled lands of Italy, Hungary, and Bohemia. Both he and the emperor Francis I were fanatically opposed to anything that smacked of liberal reforms, and as a result the Austrian government virtually stagnated during the thirty-three years, 1815–1848, known as the "age of Metternich."

Francis I no longer styled himself Holy Roman Emperor of the German Nation; under the pressure of Napoleonic change he had himself declared "Emperor of Austria" in 1806. This title substitution, however, made no practical difference in the lives of his subjects. In fact, with Metternich running the government, Austria became one of the most tightly controlled police states of nineteenth-century Europe. The prince's secret agents were everywhere, sampling public opinion and ferreting out subversive activities. An old conspirator himself, Metternich thought he could detect conspiracies in every corner of the empire.

So long as the system prevailed, Austria was to have no free press, no free parliament, no free educational institutions, and no intelligent civil service: all power was concentrated in Metternich's hands.

Despite their disappointed expectations, the Viennese learned to live with the system. Biedermeier Vienna has been called an introspective society—introspective by necessity since there were no approved political outlets for the energies and dissatisfactions of ordinary people. As in earlier epochs they took refuge in doublethink and dissimulation: Franz Grillparzer, the foremost dramatist of the age, wrote a comedy whose hero achieves his ends by always telling the truth, whereas everyone else always expects him to be lying. Grillparzer himself eventually discovered the virtues of quietly bearing the burdens of life. Like the original Viennese philosopher, Marcus Aurelius, he decided that the way to achieve true happiness lay in being content with one's lot—a Biedermeier ethic that regarded earthly ambition as pure vanity. What really mattered was *"des Innern stiller Frieden und die schuldbefreite Brust"*— "peace within oneself, and a soul freed of guilt." Even so, Grillparzer and every other intellectual worth his salt secretly or openly chafed at the restrictions and stupidities of government censorship.

Even quite ordinary, unpolitical visitors from abroad found that the activities of the Austrian police were more than slightly annoying. "Of all the troublesome cities to travelers this is surely the worst," wrote Mary Novello, the wife of Vincent Novello, a British publisher, in her diary of a journey to Vienna in the summer of 1829. "Pestered at the gates with searching the luggage; fretted with impertinent questions by the police respecting your age, station and fortune; and, to crown all, insulted by a *permit* to remain a stated time in their trumpery

The Waltz Kings

city, which if you exceed, you are likely to visit the interior of their well-contrived prisons . . . but to make up for the little provocations upon entering this capital, it must be confessed that the inhabitants are very friendly and hospitable."

The Novellos were on a "Mozart pilgrimage." They had come from London to look for vestiges of the composer whose music they loved, and in both Vienna and Salzburg they encountered many people who had known Mozart, including his widow and his aged sister. More and more foreigners— the sort of people who had paid starry-eyed visits to Beethoven a few years earlier—were coming to Vienna on such pilgrimages, to search for relics of Mozart, Haydn, and Beethoven. If they were lucky they might even run across an unpublished manuscript or two.

It was in this fashion that many of Schubert's finest works came to light, including the "Great C Major" and the "Unfinished" Symphony. One of the more persistent Schubert archaeologists was Robert Schumann, the last of the great Biedermeier romantics of music. But Schumann himself turned down the chance to follow in Beethoven's footsteps and become a resident of Vienna; a small town in Germany seemed more congenial. The Austrian capital, he decided after a visit in 1838, was no longer receptive to serious musicians; instead, most of the resident musicians were scrabbling about in the lighter sorts of music "like flies in buttermilk." Indeed, since the death of Schubert in 1828, Vienna no longer possessed a major composer-in-residence, and the memory of its great masters was

being very badly served. "Vienna is the city where Beethoven lived; and there is perhaps no place in the world where Beethoven is so little played and mentioned as Vienna. There they fear everything new, every departure from the lazy old rut," Schumann declared in his avant-garde magazine, the *Neue Zeitschrift für Musik.*

Frederic Chopin, too, had come to Vienna, in 1831, as a young composer in search of a domain in which to exercise his talents. He found, to his disappointment, that there was nothing to keep him there. His kind of music was still cultivated mainly by amateurs, the *Gesellschaft der Musikfreunde,* whose performances were so lackluster that Schubert had once left the hall in the middle of one of his own works. Still, it was considered "a gladdening sight to see counts and tradesmen, superiors and sub-alterns, professors and students, noble ladies and simple burghers' daughters side by side harmoniously exerting themselves for the love of art." The trouble was, there was no money to be made at amateur concerts. As for the professional establishment, it lived on waltzes until the latter half of the century.

The city's musical and social life now revolved, literally, around the two rival waltz conductors, Josef Lanner and Johann Strauss the Elder. They had begun their careers playing together in Lanner's tiny band, Lanner on the violin, Strauss on the viola; there was also a second violin, a guitar, and a cello. During the 1820s the group became immensely popular and grew into an orchestra of more than thirty. Under Lanner's baton, it played in tav-

Under the benevolent rule of Emperor Francis I, the man of the hour in the 1830's was Johann Strauss the Elder, who was able to ravish the easygoing Viennese with his music and his powerful band. A contemporary lithograph (below) depicts the wild dancing to Strauss's **Grand Galop** in the great hall of the Sperl in Leopoldstadt. Strauss, with his violin, conducts the huge orchestra from a podium in the balcony, while below the onlookers are kept safely isolated from the frenzied swirl of the dancers. The elder Strauss played for the "establishment" but his son Johann Strauss the Younger supported the uprising of 1848, turning out marches and polkas with revolutionary titles. His talent far outstripped that of his father, and he soon became known as the Waltz King of the World, the caption of the drawing by Theo Zasche shown at the right.

erns and coffee houses, as well as in the city's splendid amusement park, the Prater.

At first it was only Lanner who composed the new numbers for their dance repertoire; later Strauss, who was three years his junior, had to help supply the demand. In 1825 they had a falling-out at the ballroom *Zum Bock* ("At the Sign of the Ram") which ended with the two composers attacking each other with their fiddle bows—though Lanner, in a calmer moment, commemorated the occasion with a musical "lament" entitled *Trennungs-walzer* ("Separation Waltz"). The son of a glove-maker, Lanner was a gifted, self-taught composer who transformed the primitive waltz (eight bars, repeated and then transposed) into a capacious and versatile vehicle capable of expressing the gaiety and brilliance which the lighthearted Viennese reserved for their social and private lives. Even Schubert admired his waltzes and kept coming back to the tavern where Lanner's orchestra provided the music. But soon it was Strauss who became the public favorite. He adapted Lanner's lyric style to a more robust, compelling kind of waltz. The Viennese had a saying: "With Lanner it's 'Pray dance, I beg you'; with Strauss, 'You must dance, I command you!'"

Strauss had formed the nucleus of his own orchestra with fourteen of Lanner's best musicians, and he became the main drawing card of the *Sperl*, in Leopoldstadt, with its dance halls and gardens: "Strauss and his waltzes obscure everything," wrote Chopin irritably, though he himself was soon to write waltzes of his own that were veritable tone-poems in miniature. The writer Heinrich Laube arrived from Germany in 1833 and described the crowded scene at the *Sperl* when Strauss conducted there in the early summer, while the gardens were in bloom. It was, he said, "the key to Vienna as a city of pleasure":

The garden is illuminated by a thousand lamps, all the halls are open. Strauss is directing the dance music. Fire balls are everywhere, the shrubberies are alive with people and crowds are still pouring in from the city.... Under illuminated trees and in open arcades people are seated at innumerable tables eating and drinking, chattering, laughing and listening. In their midst is the orchestra from which come the new waltzes, the bugbear of our learned musicians, the new waltzes that stir the blood like the bite of a tarantula. In the middle of the garden on the orchestra platform there stands the modern hero of Austria, *le Napoléon autrichien,* the musical director, Johann Strauss.... The man is black as a Moor; his hair is curly, his mouth is melodious, energetic, his lip curls, his nose is snub; if his face were not so white he would be the complete king of the Moors....

The first part of the evening was intended mainly for eating, drinking, and listening, and Strauss would conduct the "desert storms" of his waltzes in a whirlwind of choreographic gestures. "His fiddle bow dances with his arms; the tempo animates his feet; the melody waves champagne glasses in his face," wrote Laube.

When he conducted potpourris of his favorite waltzes and polkas, the audience would greet each well-known melody with thunderous applause. So long as this part of the entertainment continued, people in the listening crowds would jostle one another and, as Laube noted, "the girls warm and laughing push their way among the lively youths." The Viennese, normally inclined to formality and politeness, did not mind bumping into each other in these circumstances. "No one apologizes; at the *Sperl* no pardon is asked or given":

And now begin the preparations for the real dancing. To keep the unruly crowds back, a long rope is put up and all who remain in the center of the hall are separated from the actual dancers. The boundary, however, is fluctuating and flexible; it is only possible to distinguish the dancers by watching the girls' heads in steady rotation. The couples waltz straight through any accidental hindrances in their joyful frenzy.... Very characteristic is the beginning of each dance. Strauss intones his trembling preludes; panting for full expression, they sound tragic.... The male partner tucks his girl deep in his arm and in the strangest way they sway into the measure.... The actual dance begins with whirling rapidity and the couple hurls itself into the maelstrom.

These sessions lasted into the early hours of the morning: "then Austria's musical hero packs up his violin and goes home to sleep a few hours and to dream of new battle stratagems and waltz themes." The Viennese adored the man and his music; he was "the waltz king" (like his son after him), a *"Melodiengott,"* and "an undeniable genius," admired all the more because in private life he was "modest, silent and attentive." He took his twenty-eight-man orchestra on tours of Europe and taught Berlin, Paris, and London what it was like to dance to an authentic Viennese waltz. The foremost French composer of the century, Hector Berlioz, attended some of his Paris performances—he gave eighty-six concerts in three months—and praised Strauss in his newspaper reviews for these exciting waltzes in which "the melody, self-intoxicated, chases and whips up the tempo."

Strauss had a genius for topicality and a knack for adapting well-known melodies to the rhythms of his waltzes, polkas, marches, and quadrilles. Among his 150 waltzes there are adaptations of themes and arias by Franz Liszt, Vincenzo Bellini, and Giacomo Meyerbeer, and even a *Cäcilien-Walzer* based on melodies from Beethoven's *Kreuzer* Sonata. He made a point of keeping his waltzes as up to date as the latest dispatches in the Viennese newspapers. Every public occasion had its special waltzes, but most especially the events on the Habsburg court calendar: weddings, coronations, baptisms, name days. Celebrities like Jenny Lind and Fanny Elssler were greeted with Strauss waltzes written in their honor. He was a very modern composer with a flair for fashion and publicity. He brought Vienna to the rest of Europe and, in turn, gave the Viennese glimpses of the other capitals he had visited—in the form of a *Carnival in Paris* gallop,

a *Brussels Lace* waltz, and *Souvenirs of Berlin* in three-quarter time. The first railroads were transforming the face of Europe: Strauss composed an *Eisenbahn-Lust Walzer,* Opus 89, that illustrated its theme, "The Joys of Railway Travel," by recreating the rattle of the wheels against the rails and the hissing of the steam locomotive.

The construction of the railroads was, in fact, an epochal event in the history of Vienna: a vast rail network was added to the traditional pattern of river and road transportation. Henceforth the city was to be more important than ever as a gateway to, and from, eastern Europe. But the public's first experience with this new and noisy means of locomotion was less than reassuring to those who were frightened of it as a possible invention of the devil. There were so many accidents on the *Kaiser-Ferdinands-Nordbahn* (the Northern Line named for the new, simple-minded emperor Ferdinand, who had ascended the throne in 1835) that Grillparzer was moved to suggest that "a hospital for invalids should be erected next to the station in the Prater." For the convenience of the passengers, he wrote, a priest and two surgeons should be kept in readiness at every station. And in another of his many railway satires, he proposed that the two railroad-development millionaires, Baron von Rothschild and Baron von Sina should resolve their rivalry over which had the better locomotives by dispatching "two trains, one from Vienna in the direction of Brünn [Brno], the other from Brünn toward Vienna, and the impact will decide which was the stronger, and demolished more of the other."

But these new, swifter means of traveling from one part of the empire to another only intensified the problem of satisfying the nationalist aspirations of its various ethnic minorities. Metternich's grip was loosening. The revolution he had feared and tried to prevent finally broke out in 1848, when Vienna first experienced the full fury of a popular uprising. Workers and students took to the streets, a unit of Viennese grenadiers sided with the rebels, a minister was lynched by the mob. Suddenly the whole city was in rebel hands. The students, chafing at the lack of academic freedom, had formed an alliance with the workers of the Vienna-Gloggnitz railway. The workers, led by members of the "Academic Legion," marched through the streets brandishing sledge hammers, spades, and red banners. The revolutionaries supported the demands of the Hungarian nationalist leader, Lajos Kossuth, for radical reforms, beginning with a written constitution. Prince Metternich announced his retirement after forty years in office. The Habsburg family fled to Innsbruck, leaving the revolutionaries in control of Vienna throughout the summer.

The Bohemians, Hungarians, and Italians had all revolted at the same time, but now the forces of the old order regained control: General Windischgraetz used artillery to restore order in Prague, while Marshal Radetzky routed the Piedmontese at the battle of Custozza. In the autumn, Windischgraetz arrived with an army drawn from the Austrian occupation forces in northern Italy. Like Napoleon, he shelled the city, and Vienna again capitulated, this time to the Austrian army. Later the Hungarian

uprising was brutally suppressed by Croatian troops of the Austrian army (who had old scores to settle with the Hungarians) and by 200,000 Russian soldiers supplied by the czar in a gesture of imperial solidarity. By then, wiser heads among the Habsburgs had decided, at Olmütz, that the amiably half-witted emperor Ferdinand must abdicate in favor of his eighteen-year-old nephew, Franz Joseph, who was expected to bring a breath of fresh air to the government of Austria.

In point of fact, the young emperor turned out to be a ruler of almost czarist conservatism, but he represented a much-needed element of stability in an empire that continued to be threatened by decay and dissolution. His reign was to last almost seventy years, until his death in 1916—longer than any other monarch's since Louis XIV. During that time the population of Vienna grew from 350,000 to two million, and the city burst out of the confinement of its Baroque shell to become a modern metropolis.

The most dramatic symbol of the profound changes that were taking place was the demolition of the old medieval ramparts, and the absorption of the old open glacis and parade ground into the Ringstrasse, a broad, stately avenue lined with imposing neo-Renaissance buildings that proclaimed the increasing power and affluence of the middle class. Professor Carl E. Schorske of Princeton has included a socio-psychological analysis of the Ringstrasse in his collection of essays, *Fin-de-siècle Vienna.* He points out that the old inner city was dominated by symbols of the court, the aristocracy, and the

church—the Hofburg, the princely palaces, St. Stephen's Cathedral, and a host of smaller churches, while the new Ringstrasse development "celebrated in architecture the triumph of constitutional *Recht* over imperial *Macht,* of secular culture over religious faith."

Vienna had become a self-governing municipality in 1850 for the first time since the imposition of Habsburg rule; in 1860, the whole of Austria exchanged constitutional government for Habsburg absolutism, following the embarrassing defeats of the army in Italy by France and Piedmont. Significantly, the Ringstrasse represented a sort of enlightened compromise between the conflicting claims of the army and the civilian interests, who were engaged in a tug of war over this enormous tract of open land encircling the old city. The army wanted the broadest possible avenue to facilitate the movement of men and equipment against potential rebels, notably the restless proletariat of the outer suburbs. The civilians wanted space to project the public image of their prosperity, and room for profitable real estate development. "Military considerations thus converged with civilian desires for an imposing boulevard to give the Ringstrasse both its circular form and its monumental scale," according to Professor Schorske.

In due course, thanks to a liberal-dominated city council, the Ringstrasse was to accommodate the most important buildings of the new "constitutional" Vienna: the University, the Parliament building, the Rathaus (town hall), and the Burgtheater (then called the Hofburgtheater, since it was still part

In this bird's-eye view of Vienna, dated 1873, the wide horseshoe-shaped swath of parks and buildings that is the Ringstrasse can be clearly traced around the Inner City, each end terminating at the Danube Canal, visible across the middle distance. Although this wash drawing by Gustav Veith was executed only thirteen years after the first announcement of the gigantic urban plan, a surprising number of buildings are already in place, especially along the left. Clearly visible are the Natural History and Kunsthistorisches museums facing the Hofburg. The confrontation of centers of culture and government on the one hand, and the residence of the emperor on the other, were to make the Ringstrasse symbolic of the new middle class's challenge to the traditional absolutism of the Habsburgs.

of the imperial court establishment), as well as the city's smartest shops and most fashionable apartment houses. Collectively, the Ringstrasse became "the pride of Vienna." At its western extension, the Opern-Ring, stands what many people still regard as the most important building in Vienna, the State Opera—then the Hofoper, or Court Opera. Erected in the 1860s, the Hofoper became the most important opera house of German-speaking Europe. It rivaled not only the Paris Opéra and La Scala, Milan, but also the Metropolitan Opera, New York, in the brilliance of its productions. The painter Moritz von Schwindt (whose chief claim to fame was that he had been a friend of Schubert's as a young man) decorated it with *Kitsch* murals of scenes from *The Magic Flute*. It was here in this immense masonry palace that some of the great battles of the Viennese *Zeitgeist* were to be fought out in the ensuing decades.

The Revolution of 1848 and the coronation of Franz Joseph were accompanied by change and succession in another Viennese dynasty—the Strauss family. At an early and indecisive stage of the uprising, Johann Strauss the Elder had composed the *Radetzky March* in honor of the imperial field marshal who had defeated the Piedmontese. It happened to be the most brilliant and memorable of his marches, and henceforth became the symbol of all that was dashing and gallant about the old Habsburg system—but for better or worse (and more by accident than design) it placed him firmly on the side of the royalists. Only after it was written did it become clear to Strauss that it had made

him persona non grata with popular audiences throughout the empire. And, shortly after writing it, Strauss died, struck down by scarlet fever just before he was to conduct the *Radetzky March* for the old soldier himself at a victory banquet held in September 1848.

He was promptly succeeded as "waltz king" by Johann Strauss the Younger, the oldest of his sons, who had become a composer and conductor against his father's wishes—and whose melodic gifts were in every way superior. Since he had sided with the revolutionaries, the younger Strauss was not accorded his father's title, Imperial and Royal Court Music Director—though he was, in fact, placed in charge of the orchestra at the great coronation ball of April 1854, at which the court celebrated Franz Joseph's wedding to his stunningly beautiful cousin, Elisabeth of Bavaria. Strauss's dramatic and immensely popular waltzes—some of them almost symphonic in breadth and scope—became the hallmark of the new, glittering Vienna that was known in the nineteen century as "the world in which no one is bored."

In retrospect, the new Vienna's formal balls and banquets have the look of scenes from comic opera, for most of the men were dressed in the gorgeous peacock uniforms with which Franz Joseph tried to maintain the illusion that Austria-Hungary was still a military power to be reckoned with. Thus, in the classic picture of the Viennese waltzing couple of the Franz Joseph era, the man wears a uniform and the woman is arrayed in a low-cut ballgown with a crinoline skirt. Ordinary people still danced, too, of course, at the Prater and at public ballrooms—to the young Strauss's immensely topical and often rather chauvinistic waltzes: the *Morning Papers* Waltz (written for the Vienna Press Association's annual ball), the *Blue Danube, Tales from the Vienna Woods, Artist's Life, Emperor Waltz,* and all the rest of them. They were soon followed by the most popular numbers from his operettas, including *Die Fledermaus* and *The Gypsy Baron.* Like his father, he toured the whole of Europe as Austria's "most successful ambassador," and he went even further afield, visiting the United States in 1876 to conduct huge concerts in New York and Boston celebrating the centenary of American independence.

Meanwhile, the flourishing Vienna of the Ringstrasse had also produced a larger and more discerning audience for symphonic music. At mid-century, the Philharmonic Orchestra brought a new professionalism to the orchestral scene, and its Sunday-morning subscription series, conducted by Otto Dessoff during the 1860s and 1870s, did much to reestablish the city's tarnished reputation for musical excellence. By the same token, important young composers, such as Johannes Brahms and Anton Bruckner, were once more coming to Vienna to live.

The young Brahms made his Viennese debut in 1862 and decided to stay on after a season as conductor of the Singakademie choir. From the first he felt at home in this city, which seemed so much more good-natured and easygoing than his native Hamburg, and he became very fond of strolling

through the Prater, particularly the *Würstelprater,* a children's playground where one could not only buy *Würstel* (sausages) but watch all sorts of shows and entertainments, including a Hungarian gypsy band whose *csardases* may well have influenced Brahms's *Hungarian Dances.*

The city's most important music critic, Edouard Hanslick, wasted no time in telling his readers that this quiet and unassuming northerner was worthy of continuing the apostolic succession of Haydn, Mozart, and Beethoven. "Brahms's close affinity with Beethoven must become clear to every musician who has not already perceived it," he wrote in the influential *Neue Freie Presse* after the première of Brahms's First Symphony. "No composer has yet approached so nearly to the great works of Beethoven as Brahms in the finale of the C Minor Symphony."

Of course there were also dissenting voices. At the première of Brahms's *A German Requiem* in 1867, he was greeted with hisses as well as applause— "a requiem on the decorum and good manners of a Vienna concert-room which astonishes and grieves us," as Hanslick wrote in his most schoolmasterish manner. Brahms's friend Theodor Billroth, one of the city's leading surgeons, decided that the young composer had "too little of the sensuous" in his art to please Viennese tastes: "His Requiem is so nobly spiritual and so Protestant-Bachish that it was difficult to make it go down here. The hissing and clapping became really violent; it was a party conflict. In the end the applause conquered."

During the 1870s the bitter feud between the followers of Richard Wagner and the partisans of Brahms tended to split the Viennese musical world into two unforgiving camps, but the majority sided with Hanslick, for whom Brahms could do no wrong and Wagner rarely anything right. They looked on Brahms, with civic pride, as their foremost genius-in-residence; indeed, *Der* Brahms with all his eccentricities became an object of public wonderment and admiration just as *Der* Beethoven had been. Surprisingly enough, this most serious of "classical" composers was also passionately fond of Viennese light music. "You must go to the Volksgarten on Friday evening when Johann Strauss will conduct the orchestra," Brahms told visiting friends. "*There* is a master; such a master of the orchestra that one never loses a single tone of any instrument." Brahms's admiration for Johann Strauss the Younger was warmly reciprocated, though it was said that when they were together it was like seeing a bear and a butterfly going for a stroll. Strauss dedicated one of his finest waltzes—*Seid Umschlungen, Millionen*—to Brahms, and frequently invited him to his summer house in Ischl, where Brahms also spent many of his holidays. When Strauss's stepdaughter, Alice, asked Brahms to sign her autograph fan, he wrote down the first bars of the *Blue Danube* and added, "Unfortunately not by Johannes Brahms!"

On the other hand, Brahms always maintained an icy reserve toward his other great contemporary, Anton Bruckner, who wrote immensely long and complex symphonies that sounded sufficiently Wagnerian to endear him to the Wagnerites. Bruckner,

Johannes Brahms, the northerner from Hamburg who moved to Vienna when he was twenty-six, immediately took a liking to the city's carefree gaiety. His classically poised music, soon recognized as in the tradition of Haydn and Beethoven, was in sharp contrast to the vertiginous melodies of Johann Strauss the Younger. Yet Brahms had a penchant for Strauss's music—no less than for that of the Hungarian gypsy bands he heard in the Prater—and the two became close friends. Brahms was a frequent visitor at Strauss's villa at Bad Ischl in the Tyrol, where the two were photographed on the garden terrace in September 1894 (left). Brahms is seen having coffee with Strauss's wife Adele at right.

who was nine years older than Brahms, had come to Vienna from Linz to serve as one of the three organists of the court chapel. After a time, however, his services were rarely called on, for he had the absent-minded habit of losing himself in his improvisations on the preludes and interludes, completely forgetting that the priests and their royal congregation were trying to finish the mass.

Bruckner taught music theory at the Vienna Conservatory and also at the University of Vienna, where his admirers included the most gifted composers of the younger generation, Gustav Mahler and Hugo Wolf. Later, when Wolf served as critic for the *Wiener Salonblatt* (1884–1887), he took up the cudgels for Bruckner and used them to belabor Brahms. "The art of composing without ideas has decidedly found its most worthy representative in Brahms," he declared.

Still, even these petty rivalries and irritations merely confirmed the fact that Viennese musical life was sufficiently robust and healthy to support more than one faction—three or four, in fact—and that modern music was moving with the times. The great art form of Vienna was undergoing the same profound and far-reaching changes that would soon produce revolutions in painting and sculpture, as well as in architecture, literature, philosophy, and science. The liberal-bourgeois optimism that had created the Ringstrasse also manifested itself in the realm of art and intellect. Though the old aristocracy had been replaced, as patrons and employers, by the wealthy middle class, Vienna then clearly began to rival Paris as an environment in which

not only music but also poetry and painting could flourish.

It was clear to most people that the days of the old Habsburg empire were numbered, yet here in the capital of this ancient monarchy the creative currents were running stronger than ever. Though Brahms had doubts and concerns about his world, he expressed them in works that were reassuring by their very eloquence—the *Alto Rhapsody,* for instance, whose message of somber compassion touched him so profoundly that he liked to keep the score under his pillow at night.

Of course there were also more vulgar manifestations of the city's red-plush affluence—the architecture of luxury hotels like the Sacher, for example, where everything was gilded, lacquered, and decked out with Oriental carpets and crystal chandeliers. The Brahms era was also the epoch of the *Göttinnen,* the much-painted and photographed "goddesses," drawn from both the *haut monde* and the demimonde: Princess Clotilde Dietrichstein, Charlotte Wolter of the Burgtheater, and Rosa Schaffer, a girl from the suburbs who became the favorite model of Hans Makart, the society painter who produced Rubens-like celebrations of buxom Viennese womanhood. It was no wonder that, as the rest of the world grew increasingly commercial and industrialized, the whole of Europe looked to Vienna for art and music, and for new wine in old bottles. As Egon Friedell wrote in one of his essays on modern culture, Vienna had become "an enclave of that vanished beauty-in-life to which so many look back with nostalgia."

Wilhelm Gause's painting of a ball in the resplendent setting of the Hofburg Palace dates from about 1890. The aging emperor Franz Joseph in his white-coated military uniform covered with medals is shown dutifully receiving the bows of beautiful young ladies. The occasion is probably the court ball attended by only the the highest civilian and military dignitaries to celebrate the Jubilee Year of 1888, the fortieth anniversary of Franz Joseph's accession to the throne. For that occasion Johann Strauss had composed his poetic and prophetically haunting **Emperor Waltz,** *expressing his deep affection for the emperor as well as his premonition of this buoyant society's doom.*

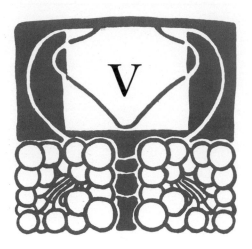

Critics and historians have been struck by the seeming paradox of the "golden age" of Vienna—that the decay of the old empire coincided with a brilliant flowering of arts and ideas that made this one of the most exciting periods in the whole of Western civilization. The phrase, "Vienna, 1900" is shorthand for a constellation of luminaries—Sigmund Freud, Gustav Mahler, Gustav Klimt, Karl Kraus, Peter Altenberg, Hugo von Hofmannsthal, Arthur Schnitzler—whose collective accomplishment was nothing less than a cultural renaissance comparable to that of Italy, but compressed into two or three decades.

They themselves were rarely aware of the tremendous potency of their epoch—they tended to see their time as only the tag-end of a great tradition. Karl Kraus described Vienna as "an experimental station for the collapse of mankind." There was some truth to this; certainly the collapse of the old gentlemanly Habsburg values was at hand, soon to be replaced by the machine-gun realities of World War I. One did not have to be much of a prophet to realize that time was out of joint, though Franz Joseph continued to reign, seemingly forever. Like Queen Victoria in England, he survived politics and natural disasters, a portrait on the post-office wall, a totem of stability in a world of uncertainties. Franz Joseph's Vienna was remote from the rather desperate doings of workaday Vienna, where one could go bankrupt so easily, or fail to find employment, or get into trouble with the police.

The literati—that is, those members of the society whose vocation it was to set things down on paper that the others only thought or felt—were assailed at every turn by doubts and fears about the future of mankind. "Somewhere there lurks a grim Fate, which may enter upon the scene at any moment," wrote the novelist Robert Musil. "It might simply be death, or it might be something else, something unimaginable, which Fate has up its sleeve. Destiny bides its time. . . ." The same sense of foreboding led another leading Viennese writer, Hermann Bahr, to suggest that his generation was teetering on the edge of an abyss: "Our epoch is shot through with a wild torment, and the pain has become no longer bearable. The cry for salvation is universal; the crucified are everywhere. Is this, then, the great death which has come upon the world?"

Yet three generations later the world looks back on Bahr, Kraus, Musil, and their contemporaries with undisguised nostalgia for this immensely creative time, which laid the foundations of modernism in the twentieth century. On second thought, there is no real contradiction between their despair and our admiration. As the Danish philosopher Søren Kierkegaard points out at the beginning of his extraordinary statement of the human condition, *Either/Or:* "What is a poet? An unhappy man who in his heart harbors a deep anguish, but whose lips are so fashioned that the moans and cries which pass over them are transformed into ravishing music."

The Viennese literati sat in their well-appointed cafés—notably the Café Griensteidl, which was torn down in 1896, and the Café Central—and wrote

Gay Apocalypse

painfully funny commentaries on the coming apocalypse; their "cosmic disquiet" *(das Kosmische Unbehagen)* runs through their novels, plays, and essays like a Wagnerian leitmotif. "There are writers who can only produce their quota of copy at the Café Central," testified Alfred Polgar, one of the youngest writers to be entitled to a place of respect in the literary cafés. "There are poets and other industrious people who receive inspiration only at the Central." The old world is coming to an end; let us drink another *Kaffee* and write a *feuilleton* on the subject.

The literary café, where reputations were made and demolished, was a remarkable institution, indispensable to the cliquish Bohemia of this increasingly crowded capital. It combined many of the functions performed for other occupations by the stock exchange, the nerve clinic, the soup kitchen, and the house of assignation. As Polgar described it in his *Theorie des Cafés Central*:

> The Café Central is not a café like other cafés, but a *Weltanschauung*, a philosophical attitude and a way of looking at the world whose very essence consists of navel-gazing and not looking at the world. The Café Central lies at the Viennese latitude, on the meridian of loneliness. Its inhabitants are, for the most part, people who are misanthropes, and whose aversion to other people is as acute as their need for people; who want to be alone, but must have company to do so.... The habitué of the Central is a person who derives no sense of belonging from his family, profession or party; the

Café Central comes to his rescue, inviting him to join and escape.... Its customers know, love and underestimate one another. Even those who profess not to know each other regard this non-relationship as a kind of relationship; mutual dislike serves as a unifying force at the Central, a sort of camaraderie. Everyone knows about everybody. The Café Central is a village in the center of the metropolis, steaming with gossip, curiosity and slander.

The sense of alienation implicit in this account was one of the principal themes of Viennese writing at the turn of the century. It permeates the work of such authors as Bahr, Schnitzler, Kraus, and Hugo von Hofmannsthal, the young symbolist nobleman of letters who wrote that "Only the cataclysm reveals supreme ecstasy." But the foremost poet of estrangement was Peter Altenberg, a ragged writer who spent virtually his entire life in cafés and variety theaters. His real métier—almost his invention—was the inconsequential anecdote or throwaway remark, hundreds of which were then published as books. Even as collections of *aperçus* they seemed as unsubstantial as the Viennese whipped-cream desert known as *Schlagobers*. Yet Hofmannsthal, the passionate aesthete, understood from the first that there was more here than met the eye. As he said of one of Altenberg's collections of prose sketches, "the little book is governed by mysterious powers as the delicate magnet is governed by enormous forces lying in the Unknown." Altenberg held court in the cafés wearing the venerable raglan-sleeved overcoat that became his

For three hundred years, ever since the first **Kaffeehaus** *was started with coffee beans abandoned by the fleeing Turks in 1683, the Viennese coffee shop has been central to the cultural life of the city. It is a social and intellectual sanctuary where anyone can go and, for the price of a cup of coffee, sit for hours in conversation with other visitors—or read newspapers and magazines from all over the world, traditionally made available by the house. To this institution perhaps more than any other can be attributed the pervasive world outlook so characteristic of the Viennese. Late afternoon is the special time when to coffee are added the epicurean delights of Viennese pastry— with Esterházytorte, Sachertorte, crisp grape strudel, exotic strawberries* mille-feuilles, *and many others.*

97

special trademark. A Walt Whitman in a pince-nez, he led the life of a beachcomber on the quicksands of literature, dependent on charity from his friends and long-suffering publishers. Hofmannsthal tells, in his diaries, of an incident in Altenberg's life that illustrates the essential ambiguities of Viennese fin-de-siècle attitudes: they wrote of *Weltschmerz* and despair, but they wanted to go on living happily ever after.

In 1904, Altenberg's health and finances had become so desperate that his friends held a council of war to determine what could be done for the poor man. During their deliberations, the poet himself sat in an armchair, a little apart from his friends. "I am a beggar and a dying man," he said, covering his face with his hands. "What do you want from me? Just let me die in peace." Several people got up to suggest different ways in which they might help him recover his health, but Altenberg, trembling with fever, seemed to reject every offer. Then the prettiest woman present rose from her chair. "I love Altenberg more than any of you; I love his soul and the gestures of his soul. I don't know of anything more beautiful than to see him die, in a corner, covered with a threadbare blanket. The poor man! Who would want to cheat him of the beauty of his death?" At this, Altenberg jumped up from his armchair in a fit of temper. "You silly goose!" he shouted. "I don't want to die; I want to live; I want a warm room with a gas heater, an American rocking chair, a pension, orange marmalade, beef broth, filet mignon: I want to live!"

There was, indeed, a great deal of life in fin-de-siècle Vienna, despite the many pronouncements to the contrary. Never before in the course of human events had so "decadent" and pessimistic an age produced so much that was vital, optimistic, and significant for the future. It was the great germinal period of the twentieth-century arts. For that matter, the major figures in this turn-of-the-century renaissance were labeled "decadent" only by their critics; they themselves never described their work as such.

There was Gustav Klimt, for example, the leading painter of Vienna, 1900, who was attacked for painting "bodies that are tinged with the blue haze of decadence." In actual fact, he painted some of the most sinuously beautiful women's bodies of all time, and swathed them in mysterious textiles that seemed to have been woven in the dream factories of the imagination—severely geometric patterns that stand in striking contrast to the erotic naturalism of his faces and bodies. No one had ever seen pictures like these before. They have in them something of the Thousand and One Nights, combined with the meticulous realism of modern Vienna. The art critic Berta Szeps-Zuckerkandl wrote that Klimt had created a new kind of "modern" woman, "with a boyish slimness and a puzzling charm"; she was the forerunner of the breathtaking Greta Garbo type who was to bring Klimt's ideal to the cinema screens of the 1920s and 1930s.

It was largely thanks to Klimt that Vienna acquired a fin-de-siècle art capable of holding its own in competition with Paris and Brussels. His school of painting became known as the *Secession* because

he and his companions had "seceded" from the established academic traditions and institutions in order to join forces with the modernists of other nations in an effort "to show modern man his true face," as the architect Otto Wagner expressed it. The first exhibition of the Vienna *Secession,* held in the spring of 1898, included works by such foreign artists as Puvis de Chavannes, Auguste Rodin, Fernand Khnopff, Constantin Meunier, John Singer Sargent, and Frank Brangwyn. Significantly, it was Klimt who provided the most important Austrian contributions and much else besides: he was president of the artists' association and of the working committee, and designed the poster for the exhibition, a powerful drawing of Theseus slaying the Minotaur under the watchful eye of Pallas Athene. Here the censor intervened (as he still did throughout Viennese public life), because he objected to Theseus's nakedness, and Klimt was obliged to hide his loins behind a copse of overprinted trees. At least the "all-highest authority," Franz Joseph, was not overtly hostile to this new development—unlike Kaiser Wilhelm II of Germany, who made rude public statements about *"diese Dreckkunst aus Paris"* ("this filthy art from Paris") which was corrupting the tastes of all right-thinking art lovers.

The motto of the *Secession* was inscribed over the main entrance of the "temple of art" that Josef Olbrich designed for it on the Karlsplatz—"to the age, its art; to art, its freedom." The Secessionists tried to spell out their vision of the new world in a splendidly designed and illustrated magazine, *Ver Sacrum* ("Sacred Spring"), published from 1898

to 1903. It sums up the whole genius of fin-de-siècle Vienna, and counts as one of the classic "little magazines" of all time. Bahr, Altenberg, and Hofmannsthal were among the contributors, as well as Rainer Maria Rilke, Arno Holz, Otto Julius Bierbaum, Emile Verhaeren, and Richard Dehmel (the author of *Verklaerte Nacht*—"Transfigured Night"—which Arnold Schoenberg used as the basis for his first Expressionist masterpiece for strings). Besides drawing illustrations and ornaments for *Ver Sacrum,* Klimt regularly provided the most exciting new pictures for each successive exhibition of the *Secession.*

When Klimt tried to take the logical next step, however, and move from the private sphere into the public sector, he ran into powerful opposition from representatives of the status quo. The Ministry of Culture had commissioned him to provide three allegorical ceiling paintings for the ceremonial hall of the new University of Vienna—on the themes of "Philosophy," "Medicine," and "Jurisprudence." When Klimt exhibited the original version of "Philosophy" at the *Secession* in 1900, an influential group of university professors protested against the picture and petitioned the government to prevent its installation in their hall. This initial barrage touched off the greatest art scandal in the history of Vienna. The matter was taken up in Parliament and, of course, by the press: it became a cause célèbre on which everyone must needs express an opinion, informed or otherwise.

In the end, Klimt withdrew from the project. One of his wealthy patrons, August Lederer, advanced him the money to pay back the 30,000-crown ad-

100

After working on the ceiling decorations of the Burgtheater, Gustav Klimt came to realize that painting was not limited to the simple imitation of nature but was an art capable of conveying the full range of human emotions, of penetrating the innermost core of the psyche. As a metaphor of erotic power, his audacious Judith and Holofernes *painted in 1901, suggests how the inexhaustible capacity of female sexuality can threaten the male. Encased in a hieratic setting of formalized design and dress, the figure of a fashionable Viennese woman—not unlike that of some of Klimt's later portraits of society ladies—in shown full-face, triumphantly holding a decapitated head. The stark contrast between the voluptuous nude and its harsh, metallic surroundings heightens the psychological tension of the theme.*

vance he had received from the government. Lederer, in time, acquired the most important collection of Klimts in private hands, but it suffered an all-too characteristic fate. Most of the pictures were confiscated by the Nazis after the annexation of Austria in 1938, when Lederer's children had to flee the country, and during the war the canvases were burned in a fire at the château where the Nazis had stored them for "safekeeping."

Klimt, at any rate, refused to be intimidated by the academic outcry over his glowingly erotic pictures. And he continued to prefer the air of Vienna to any other artistic climate. At least, whatever the professors might have thought, the avant-garde was solidly behind him, and that included not only the poets and aesthetes but the wealthy art collectors of the Ringstrasse. It was thanks to them—and not the official establishment—that Vienna acquired its international reputation as a seedbed of the arts. Besides there were certain aspects of this city that made it particularly attractive to artistic temperaments. When Rodin visited Vienna in June 1902, to view Klimt's Beethoven frieze at the *Secession* exhibit, Berta Szeps-Zuckerkandl invited the French sculptor, together with Klimt and other members of the group, to partake of a typical Viennese *Jause* (afternoon coffee) in the Sacher garden-restaurant in the Prater.

Indeed, never before had so many gifted people practiced their arts in the Austrian capital. It was a world distinguished for its visual elegance, its literary brilliance, and its musical excellence. These were the years when Gustav Mahler presided over the fortunes of the Vienna Opera—an epoch which his assistant conductor, Bruno Walter, described in his memoirs as "a ten-year festival to which a great musician invited fellow artists and audiences." Unlike his predecessors in the great Viennese tradition, Mahler was that rare phenomenon, a great composer who was also a brilliant conductor, and who possessed the organizing ability that enabled him to direct the day-to-day affairs of a major opera house.

Vienna had never seen anything like this bundle of energy who revitalized a lackluster company and brought it to a pitch of perfection that dazzled even the most exigent critics. "He conquered Vienna with his first appearance on the podium," Walter recalled. "His dominion over audiences was unbroken to the last." The aging Brahms, who had always said that no one could conduct Mozart properly, went into ecstasies when he first heard Mahler conduct *Don Giovanni*: "Yes, that's how it has to be!—Excellent! Fabulous! What a devil of a fellow!"

Under Mahler's direction, the *Hofoper* became a focal point of interest in the arts, particularly after he called in Alfred Roller, one of the major painters of the *Secession,* to redesign the stage sets and décor of the company's major productions. The whole city talked about Mahler's régime at the opera house, and the cafés were full of gossip concerning the comings and goings of his principals. Bruno Walter writes that "as he crossed the street, hat in hand, gnawing his lip or chewing his tongue, cabmen would turn to look at him and mutter, in tones of awe 'Mahler himself!'"

No one had ever run an opera theater like this, declared Hermann Bahr; here was a company whose policies were decided by "purely artistic motives." Mahler, in fact, abolished many of the Opera's long-standing traditions because they detracted from the performances. "What you theatre-people call your tradition," he told them, "is nothing but laziness and *Schlamperei* [i.e., sloppiness, the other side of the coin of the famous Viennese *Gemütlichkeit*]." He did away with the claque of paid applause, makers who cheered the stars at so much per aria; now even the established stars had to restudy their parts and earn their applause. Performances now began on time, and latecomers were no longer permitted to disturb the others by taking their seats during the overture; instead, they had to wait outside until the next break in the performance—an unheard-of disciplinary measure in those days. He restored the music that was always cut from the Wagner operas, but by the same token he made daring innovations in the staging of Wagner and Mozart, including an Expressionist production of *Don Giovanni* which is regarded as a milestone in the annals of opera.

Mahler was famous for being utterly uncompromising in his musical standards. When one aspiring soprano came to him with a letter of recommendation from the crown prince, Franz Ferdinand, Mahler tore up the letter and snapped, "Very well, and now let's hear you sing!" Bruno Walter says that "something new and exciting was injected into the sensuous culture of the city" by Mahler's direction of the Opera, and by the exemplary intensity and dedication he brought to the task. Even Franz Joseph was delighted to tell him, during his first season, 1897–1898: "It has taken you no time at all to make yourself master of the house!"—a spontaneous tribute from one natural ruler to another.

Mahler's enthusiasm for the operas in his repertoire kept him working at a fever pitch for the better part of a decade. Walter noted that he approached every opera "like a lover, constantly wooing," and that he was always ready to "reconsider, improve, plumb new depths. Nothing was routine in his performances; even if he was giving a work for the thirtieth time, he gave it as though for the first." Yet, paradoxically, Mahler's very success as an operatic conductor militated against his career as a composer. No one was more acutely conscious of this dilemma than Mahler himself. At the opera house, he told his friend Natalie Bauer-Lechner, "I don't enjoy a particle of the satisfaction I derive from really working and composing. . . . I don't have enough time and opportunity to do the work that God meant me to do, and I don't really like living in the limelight."

He called himself a *Sommerkomponist* because he was reduced to writing his symphonies during the summer months, when the opera house was closed, and he could move to a mountain village in the Austrian Alps where there was no one to disturb him. Usually it took him two summers to complete one of his long, complex scores, and since he was an active hiker and mountaineer, these scores are full of references to nature, especially birdcalls and the sound of wind and water. "My music is always

The House of the Secession (right), designed by architect Josef Olbrichs and opened for its first exhibition in 1897, was intended as a shrine of modern art and a refuge from frozen tradition, the snaky heads of three furies over its entrance door symbols of the awakened instinctual life. For a 1902 exhibition of a much-admired statue of Beethoven by Leipzig sculptor Max Klinger, a group of Secession artists collaborated to transform their building in homage to the great composer. The interior was remodeled by avant-garde architect Josef Hoffmann, Klimt painted his Beethoven frieze, and others contributed sculptures and ceramic plaques. Gustav Mahler prepared a specially condensed arrangement of the Ninth Symphony for the opening. In the photograph above of artists who participated in this event, Klimt is seated in a throne-like chair at left.

and everywhere like a sound of nature," he once explained, and several of his symphonies are a direct evocation of the mountain landscapes that surrounded him as he wrote. The Sixth Symphony, for example, is punctuated with the sound of cowbells and suggests "the last earthly sounds heard from the valley far below by the departing spirit on the mountain top," while in the Seventh Symphony, as he says, "nature roars" in the opening movement.

Modern critics are in general agreement that Mahler was the most important composer of his time, and that he brought the symphonic tradition of Mozart-Beethoven-Brahms to a magnificent conclusion. The German composer and writer Karlheinz Stockhausen has suggested that Mahler's music mirrors the whole of creation more brilliantly than that of any other composer. If a higher being from a distant star should want to investigate the nature of the beings who inhabit our planet, he would do well to address himself to Mahler's symphonies: "In order to discover all that which is most characteristic of the earthling, to understand his entire range of passions, from the most angelic to the most animal, to know everything that binds him to the earth and lets him no more than dream of the other regions of the universe, there would be no richer source of information than Mahler."

During his own lifetime, however, Mahler encountered very little real comprehension among musical audiences. Vienna should have been the first to understand him, for although he was born in Kalischt (now Kaliste), Bohemia, he had attended the Vienna Conservatory and spent his most important years in the city. Yet, much as they admired him as conductor of the Opera and of the Vienna Philharmonic, most of the city's music lovers professed an acute dislike of his symphonies. It was the problem of Klimt and the university professors all over again. When Mahler conducted the Philharmonic in the première of his Fourth Symphony in 1902, for example, Natalie Bauer-Lechner noted that many people had attended only in order to make fun of the performance: "They laughed, and expressed their dislike in all sorts of gestures. Afterwards they stood around in groups and chattered. I heard them say, 'He starts out as though he wanted to play a carnival prank on the audience.' Others were disappointed that there hadn't been more hissing. A couple of youths said it was 'ghastly' and not really music."

This psychological block known as "the nonacceptance of the unfamiliar" was by no means an exclusively Viennese phenomenon. Auguste Rodin had encountered it in Paris when he first exhibited his "gibbous" monument to Honoré de Balzac in 1898. James Whistler experienced it in London, Richard Strauss in Munich and Berlin. It was an age of dramatic changes in the arts, and every innovation, whether undertaken by the Impressionists, Symbolists, or Expressionists, was greeted with the same hostility and derision. It was only natural, then, that the Viennese should have resisted all those who contributed most to their golden age. Mahler was ultimately driven out of the city by the machinations of his enemies. Klimt (like Rodin) chose to withdraw from the battle with an uncomprehending public: *"Ich will loskommen!"* he told Berta Szeps-Zuckerkandl. "I want to get out of this." Henceforth he took refuge in his private, mystical world of erotic women and sensuous landscapes.

Nor is it surprising that the quintessential Viennese intellectual of 1900—Sigmund Freud—should have fought the longest and hardest battle. Freud's struggle against prejudice and incomprehension lasted for more than forty years, though the whole thrust of his teaching was liberation from prejudice. Freud's discoveries "brought into the world a new definition of human fate," as his pupil Abraham Kardiner has pointed out, "because he placed in the hands of man the means with which to alter impediments which were previously considered irremediable. 'You need not be the victim of your own past,' said Freud, 'or of your own environment.'"

Freud's voyages of discovery into the dark continent of the unconscious were undertaken in the spirit of scientific inquiry, yet they had an incalculable effect not only on the behavioral sciences but also on the arts. Arnold Schoenberg and Oskar Kokoschka, as well as Franz Kafka and Max Ernst— but also Pablo Picasso, Salvador Dalí, André Gide, André Breton, Albert Camus, James Joyce, D. H. Lawrence, Virginia Woolf, Thomas Mann are all, in some measure, part of the Freudian revolution in human consciousness. Indeed, the whole of twentieth-century art is "Freudian," though the word has been applied so often and so loosely as to be almost meaningless.

According to Freud himself, his method was based on two fundamental propositions. First, "that mental processes are essentially unconscious, and that those which are conscious are merely isolated acts and parts of the whole psychic entity." And second, that "impulses which can only be described as sexual in both the narrower and the wider sense, play a peculiarly large part, never before sufficiently appreciated, in the causation of nervous and mental disorders"—though on the other hand, "these sexual impulses have contributed invaluably to the highest cultural, artistic and social achievements of the human mind."

The second of these propositions was by far the harder for his contemporaries to accept. Freud's recognition of infantile sexuality and its role in the etiology of the neuroses led him to be ostracized by the medical profession, though he always insisted that he had not revealed anything that every nursemaid didn't know. When he began writing about it, infantile sexuality was still a forbidden subject in scientific circles. As one irate psychiatrist shouted at a medical congress, "This is not a topic for discussion at a scientific meeting, it is a matter for the police!"

For many years, therefore, the Viennese regarded Freud (if they had heard of him at all) as little more than a quack psychiatrist. At the age of forty, when he embarked on his epoch-making investigation of dream symbolism, he had, as he said, "reached the peak of loneliness, and had lost all my old friends and hadn't acquired any new ones; no one paid any attention to me, and the only thing

that kept me going was a bit of defiance and the beginning of *The Interpretation of Dreams.*"

His book came off the press in 1899 but bore the date 1900, as though to signalize the beginning of a new era of self-awareness. It was not long before he was surrounded by a circle of brilliant disciples, including Alfred Adler, Otto Rank, and (for a time) Carl Jung. There was a tendency to treat him as the Delphic Oracle of Vienna, especially since a conversation with Freud was considered a great intellectual adventure. "While one learned, one marveled," Stefan Zweig noted. "It was plain that one's every word was fully comprehended by this magnificent, unprejudiced person whom no admission startled, no statement excited, and whose impulse to make others see and feel clearly had long since become an instinctive life impulse." Even Gustav Mahler came to spend a day with Freud while he was in Holland on a holiday—a sort of emergency psychoanalysis that helped him function for another year while he worked on his Tenth (and Unfinished) Symphony.

Some of Freud's critics, including Jung, tried to suggest that his theories were relevant only to the Viennese-Jewish bourgeois world of which he was a product. Yet the speed with which his ideas were accepted by other nations and cultures would argue otherwise. He himself tended to be cosmopolitan in his thinking, and was always quite unflustered when he was confronted by anti-Semitism in whatever form. Born in Moravia, he had grown up in one of the poorer Jewish districts of Vienna, and had first encountered organized discrimination while he was a student at the university. At the time he had been merely angered by "the imputation that I should regard myself as inferior and not belonging to the people, just because I was a Jew. . . . I could never understand why I ought to be ashamed of my ancestry, or as people were beginning to call it, my 'race.' As to the membership in the [Austro-German] ethnic folk-community that was denied me, I relinquished my claims to it without much regret." On the contrary, religious prejudice merely encouraged him to think for himself— "As a Jew I was prepared to be in the opposition and to renounce my agreement with the 'compact majority.'"

Yet the artists and intellectuals who created the great Viennese tradition had all been outsiders and aliens in one way or another—even Beethoven and Mozart had renounced their agreement with the "compact majority." It was one of the city's great cultural resources that it was situated on the cusp where German-speaking culture intersected with the Hungarian and Czech, as well as the Yiddish, Polish, and Italian. The emancipation of the Jews of Austria in 1867 had led to a great influx of Jews from the provinces, and by the turn of the century Jews constituted about ten percent of the population. In the arts and sciences the proportion was much higher—Mahler, Kraus, Altenberg, Schnitzler, Hofmannsthal, Ludwig Wittgenstein, Schoenberg, and innumerable others all came from Jewish or partly Jewish families. They thought of themselves, however, as Viennese first and foremost. As yet, no one could foresee the time when a writer's books

The photograph below of Sigmund Freud's famous consulting office in Vienna provides an insight into the breadth of his intellectual interests. The pictures and artifacts in this cluttered bourgeois interior are there not for aesthetic display but as tokens of his preoccupation with primitive myths and religions. The large picture directly above the couch shows the temple of Rameses II at Abu Simbel; to the left, the marble head in the corner of the room recalls his deep interest in classical archaeology; even the oriental rugs lend an aura of ethnological curiosity. After Freud's long-deferred appointment to a professorship at the University of Vienna and the publication of **The Interpretation of Dreams,** *he widened his field of psychological inquiries to cultural problems. But with the advent of Hitler in 1938 the father of psychoanalysis was forced to abandon his chair at the university and, at the age of eighty-two, to board a plane bound for England (left).*

would be burned merely because his parents happened to be Jewish.

Whatever their background, it was a nation of brilliant overachievers, making the most of this great nexus of traditions. Freud's work, for example, is solidly rooted in the German classics—he was to win the Goethe prize for literary achievement—but also in the Greek and Roman, as well as Shakespeare and the great French writers. The very multiplicity of educational influences—his German training, his studies in Paris and Trieste, his early visit to England—all of these were a reflection of a typically Viennese curiosity about the world at large.

Of course there were tensions among the various groups that made up this cauldron of cultures. Robert Musil satirized them in *The Man Without Qualities,* when he suggested that even ethnic prejudices might have had some positive function: "it was not only dislike of one's fellow citizens that was intensified into a strong sense of community; even mistrust of oneself and of one's own destiny here assumed the character of profound self-certainty." No one will deny that it was a society fraught with paradoxes, but by the same token it produced an era of astonishing brilliance whose influence on the rest of the century has not yet been fully appreciated in the English-speaking world. This fin-de-siècle Vienna has been described as "a beacon of modernity in a drifting world." Hermann Broch, one of the great Viennese writers of the next generation, summed it up perfectly when he called it "the gay Apocalypse."

VI

The dance on the brink of a volcano, as it came to be called, was never irresponsible or unconscious. Viennese artists and intellectuals were far more aware than their French or Italian contemporaries that they were destined to witness a great upheaval. The Expressionists and Modernists did their utmost to avert the disaster by trying to teach the world something about humanism and the brotherhood of man. Franz Werfel, one of the many Prague-born poets who came to Vienna with the generation of 1910, begins his poem *Der Weltfreund* (Friend of the World) with the lines "My only desire, oh Man, is to be kin to thee!"—an Expressionist echo of the lines that Beethoven had set to music in the finale of the Ninth Symphony: "*Seid umschlungen, Millionen*" ("Let me embrace you, millions of mankind!"). The Viennese writer Stefan Zweig remembered that before World War I there was hardly a city in Europe "where the drive towards cultural ideals was as passionate as it was in Vienna." Although the aging emperor was never to be seen except in army uniform and everyone at court followed suit, it was tacitly understood that these gorgeous costumes in red and white and blue with gleaming buttons and golden epaulettes were meant to be worn on dress parades or at the opera ball—and never for anything as serious as a military campaign. Vienna, Zweig wrote, was an epicurean city, and "what is culture, if not to wheedle from the coarse material of life, by art and love, its finest, its most delicate, its most subtle qualities?" Hence its young men danced the nights away; they went to the theater and to the city's magnificent res-

taurants, with the most cosmopolitan cuisine in the world; they flocked to art galleries and listened to Karl Kraus, the funniest and most serious critic who ever lived, read from his own and other people's poetry.

The rest of Europe marveled at the tenacity and persistence with which Franz Joseph maintained the courtly traditions of another age. In 1910, Guillaume Apollinaire wrote glowingly about the Carnival ball soon to take place at Schoenbrunn—a court ball in miniature to which the emperor had invited all the children belonging to the imperial family. "The House of Habsburg-Lorraine is rich in children, and there will be not less than fifty-two couples at the ball. All the rules of court etiquette will be scrupulously observed, and the little archduchesses will do the honors, serving tea at the different tables. The 'first lady of the court' will be the lovely little Archduchess Ella, granddaughter of the emperor. And if any of the guests does not behave like a perfect courtier he will receive a good spanking."

It seemed, at the time, that this quaintly charming state of affairs would last forever; at any rate, after more than sixty years of rule, Franz Joseph showed no signs of faltering. He lived in Olympian isolation, a man of "sparse humanity," as Hermann Broch described him, imprisoned in a vast shell of solitude, "in which he lived his uncannily bureaucratic, abstractly punctual life of a civil servant." He was the very opposite of a *Volkskaiser* (an emperor "of the people"), yet his subjects in both halves of the Dual Monarchy, Austria-Hungary, admired him pre-

The Phoenix Rises

cisely because he had taken on himself "the awe-inspiring dignity of absolute loneliness."

Socially, Franz Joseph was the most exclusive of Habsburg emperors. He did not condescend to mix with the great nobles of the realm, only with other members of the imperial house—the fifty-six archdukes and archduchesses who had all been raised in the same strict school of service to the empire. Then, suddenly, the assassination of Archduke Franz Ferdinand, the emperor's nephew and heir to the throne, plunged Europe into war. The decision to "punish" Serbia was Franz Joseph's own: ultimately, it was he himself who set a match to the powder keg that exploded the empire.

There had been local wars since the time of Metternich, but no one was prepared for the great pan-European conflict that followed the assassination. At the beginning, in August and September 1914, there was so much enthusiasm for the monarchy that the authorities were taken by surprise. The Czechs, Hungarians, Slovenes, and other "tribes" of the empire suppressed their nationalist rivalries in a rare display of patriotic solidarity. As the troops moved toward the front, they were cheered on by the local population. "The behavior of the populace, of all nationalities, was the best conceivable," reported a staff officer of the Austrian Fourth Army. "Patriotic feeling was everywhere in evidence, and at the larger stations the troops were given bread, tea, cigarettes, etc. by women of all classes."

The fighting at the front, however, took a heavy toll of the professional officers, who had cultivated good relations with their men and gone to the trouble of learning their languages. The professionals were replaced by reserve officers, mainly German-Austrians and Hungarians, who tended to be arrogant and patronizing toward the minorities in the ranks. Henceforth "the Good Soldier Schweik" and thousands like him tried their best to do as little as possible without actually being shot for malingering. Morale in the army had collapsed by the time the emperor died, in 1916, though his state funeral was the occasion for one last splendid march-past of the Dual Monarchy's gorgeously attired Guards regiments. A new emperor, Karl, succeeded to the throne, but the Viennese were too hungry to cheer; they realized even then that the war was lost.

Much as the Austrian government would have liked to do so, it was now too late to arrange a negotiated settlement: the insane bloodletting would have to continue until the armies of Austria and Germany were wholly exhausted. Since the fighting took place far from the capital, it was "business as usual" in Vienna—but the ranks of those who had create the city's prewar flowering of culture were decimated. The most gifted of the young Austrian Expressionist poets, George Trakl, regarded service in the army as a kind of punishment for the accumulated sins that constituted his guilt complex: "I do not have the right to withhold myself from Hell." He was drafted into the medical corps and sent to the front in Austrian Poland, where he survived months of the bitter fighting which he managed to describe in a new kind of non-heroic war poetry:

The myth of imperial splendor maintained by
Franz Joseph until the end of his life reached
its apogee in the elaborate pageant along the
Ringstrasse to celebrate his silver wedding
anniversary in 1879. The watercolor above,
by the painter Hans Makart, shows the
emperor's coach, drawn by eight Lippizaner
stallions, leaving the Hofburg Palace on the
way to the viewing stand. Makart drew the
plans for the pageant, designed the costumes,
and led the glittering procession on a white
charger. No less splendor of dress can be seen
in the snapshot at right of the heir to the
throne, Francis Ferdinand, and his wife,
Sophie, in Sarajevo in 1914—shortly before
they were assassinated by a Bosnian student.
In 1916, the last year of his reign, the aged
Franz Joseph strolls through the formal park
at Schoenbrunn (above right).

114

With broken brows, silver arms
The night beckons dying soldiers.
In the shade of autumnal ash trees
Sigh the ghosts of slain men.

As the casualties mounted, older men well past military age were conscripted into the non-combatant units. Among them was the gentlest of Austrian lyric poets, Rainer Maria Rilke.

Arnold Schoenberg, too, was briefly drafted into the army, though he was forty-three. One of his fellow soldiers asked him whether he really was Arnold Schoenberg, the controversial composer about whom so much had been written in the newspapers. Schoenberg thought for a moment and then conceded that, yes, he was the man in question. "But see here," he added. "Somebody had to be it, though nobody wanted to be, so I agreed to give myself for the purpose."

Schoenberg's friends worked very hard to get him released from military service, and eventually he was able to return to civilian life, where he continued to develop the new theory of harmony that was gradually forming itself in his mind. His pupil Anton von Webern (exempt on account of poor eyesight) remembered going to see him in the spring of 1917: "Schoenberg lived in the Gloriettegasse and I nearby; one fine morning I went up to see him, to tell him that I had read in a newspaper where one might be able to buy some groceries. I happened to catch him at work, and he told me that he was 'on the way to an entirely new thing.' More than that he didn't tell me at the time, and

I kept asking myself, 'For heaven's sake, what could it be?'" It was the so-called twelve-tone technique, the most influential music theory of the twentieth century, which Schoenberg was not to make public until 1923—his "method of composing with twelve tones related only to one another." He was particularly proud of it because he felt it would assure the continuity of the Viennese classical tradition for another hundred years.

The end, when it came, also toppled the monarchy and dismembered the empire. Under the peace terms imposed by the victorious Allies, Austria proper was severed from its subject states and reduced to one-eighth its former size, without developed natural resources of its own. When the Provisional National Assembly proclaimed the small country a democratic republic, the young emperor Karl went into exile. Twice he was to make comic-opera attempts to regain his throne—in each case, significantly, it was the nobles of Hungary rather than Austria whom he tried to rally to his side—but in the end he was bundled off to the island of Madeira to die in the sun, like Napoleon or a retired British colonel.

Like the new Austria, postwar Vienna was only a shadow of its former self. Its acres of gray, empty palaces had lost their function; the city as a whole seemed too large to serve as a capital of so small a country. "The Czechs, Poles, Italians and Slovenes had snatched away their countries," Stefan Zweig noted. "What remained was a mutilated trunk. . . . Of the six or seven millions who were forced to call themselves 'German-Austrians,' two starving and freezing millions crowded the capital alone; the industries which had formerly enriched the land were on foreign soil, the railroads had become wrecked stumps, the State Bank received in place of its gold the gigantic burden of the war debt."

The economic chaos of the postwar decade completed the destruction of the old social order. Without gold backing, the imperial *Krone,* once one of the great currencies of Europe, became practically worthless. Austria's inflation anticipated the one that was soon to devastate the German economy. The price of an egg rose to the prewar price of an automobile; a single meal in a restaurant cost as much as a year's rent for a prewar apartment. Many members of the old middle class lost their life savings and their position in society; their place was taken by a new class of speculators and profiteers who made fortunes on the black market. Under food rationing, the average citizen was entitled to little more than a daily meal of thin vegetable soup and a piece of black bread. Everyone told stories of respectable housewives selling themselves in sleazy nightclubs in order to feed their husbands and undernourished children.

Members of the old aristocracy, whose titles were officially abolished by the republic, could count themselves fortunate if they were not forced to sell off their palaces and châteaux to foreign "tourists" who invaded Austria with their prized foreign currencies in order to buy up antiques and real estate. "Vienna is sad," wrote the (former) Princess Marie von Thurn and Taxis to Rilke, then living in Switzerland:

I think it could say, *Tout est perdu fors la musique* [All is lost except for music]. But that, thank God and touching wood, has remained and is more magnificent than ever. . . . In Vienna people talk politics a lot, criticize everything, and complain about everything; there is a great deal of dancing and dying, starving and carousing. There is hardly anyone left of our former society. The people who now pretend to represent Vienna society run after the Entente in a most undignified and tactless manner and live on the fat of the land; they are either foreign tarts or people that were hardly ever seen in former times. One has not gained by the exchange.

Culturally, too, Vienna was an alchemist's retort of changing values. Most of the city's artists and intellectuals struggled through these years of deprivation with varying degrees of success. Klimt had died in 1917, of a heart attack; his most gifted disciple, Egon Schiele, was killed by the great influenza epidemic of 1918. He had just painted the superb self-portrait that shows him nude, together with his wife and the still-imaginary figure of a young child they were expecting at the time. It was destined never to be born, for his wife also died of influenza, preceding Schiele to the grave by only three days.

Those who survived these disasters learned to adjust to the collapse of the old values. It was easier if one could muster the stoic courage of Sigmund Freud, who continued to work on the development of his psychoanalytic theories in his unheated apartment in the Berggasse, indifferent to the fact that

118

Egon Schiele, abandoning the cult of pathos and erotic introspection in which he first sought to express his anxieties, later found release in "biographical allegories." His portrait of the painter Paris von Gütersloh (left), who was to become the mainspring of the post-World-War II school of Fantastic Realists, is caught in an electrifying pose in this canvas dating from 1917, the year before Schiele died. At about the same time Arnold Schoenberg (right), then in his early forties, also was "on the way to an entirely new thing." That was his twelve-tone method of composing, which he did not make public until 1923, and which became the most influential music theory of the twentieth century.

he had lost his life savings and was trying to raise his family on vegetable soup. Arnold Schoenberg, too, stubbornly maintained his perfectionist's vision of an ideally conceived and executed modern music, though he was aware that this new era had brought "the overturning of everything one has believed in." Immediately after the war he and his disciples founded the Society for Private Musical Performance, which was intended to provide its members with showcase performances of the latest avant-garde music.

His twelve-tone system, as revealed in his own works and those of Webern and Berg, created a sensation among avant-garde musicians. In time the whole world of modern music was to split into two rival camps, the "dodecaphonic" or "serial" composers of Schoenberg's school, and all the non-converted, most of them belonging to the neoclassical or Igor Stravinsky faction (though Stravinsky himself would ultimately adopt the serial technique for some of his last works). Those who regarded the serial technique as the natural outgrowth of the classical tradition considered Schoenberg the most significant figure in twentieth-century music. His fiftieth birthday on September 13, 1924, was celebrated with a serenade at the town hall, a message from the mayor of Vienna, and a special issue of the modernist magazine, *Musikblätter des Anbruch.* Yet the official musical institutions of the city preferred to ignore him, just as the University of Vienna had snubbed Freud for many years. Somehow the Vienna Academy of Music could never find it in its heart to offer him a professorship—

though he was famous as one of the great teachers of music theory.

At least the Schoenberg school had the satisfaction of producing the most important operatic score of 1920s Vienna, Alban Berg's electrifying *Wozzeck.* Berg had seen a production of Georg Büchner's early nineteenth-century drama in Berlin just before the war. It deals with a simple-minded enlisted man in the Prussian army who is driven to murder and suicide by the cruelties and harassments of his superiors. During the war Berg himself had a taste of army life; it made him acutely sensitive to the sufferings of common soldiers, especially those of Slavic descent, in regiments commanded by German disciplinarians of the old school. As a consequence, he began composing a brilliantly Expressionist score for Büchner's text. Yet it was not in Vienna but in Berlin that *Wozzeck* had its immensely successful première. It was given in December 1925 under Erich Kleiber, who had devoted more than 130 rehearsals to getting it letter-perfect.

Early in 1926, Schoenberg left Vienna to become professor of composition at the Prussian Academy of Arts in Berlin, the most prestigious post in the German musical world. "I want to depart just as unnoticed as I always was when I lived here," he told a Viennese reporter as a Parthian shot. It was the beginning of an exodus that impoverished the intellectual life of Vienna, a long slide toward the extinction of art and ideas that culminated in the *Anschluss* and ultimately in Auschwitz. The city's most important young philosopher, Ludwig Wittgenstein, left Vienna two years later for Trinity Col-

With the collapse of the Austro-Hungarian empire and the signing of the Armistice on November 11, 1918, Charles, the last Habsburg emperor, departed and the first Austrian Republic was proclaimed. "Long Live the Socialist Republic" is the slogan on the large banner held aloft in front of the crowd at left, facing the Parliament building in Vienna in November 1918. In 1935, soon after Austrian chancellor Engelbert Dollfuss had dissolved Parliament and assumed absolute control of the government in the face of the growing Nazi menace, he was assassinated. National Socialist conspirators backed by Hitler and disguised in Austrian army uniforms forced entry into the Chancellery and also took over the radio station. The photograph at right, dated July 25, 1935 —the day Dollfuss was killed—shows the action outside the radio station on Johannes Gasse.

lege, Cambridge. He was to revolutionize philosophy much as Schoenberg had revolutionized music. The new political atmosphere had made Vienna uncomfortable for both of them, since the city's anti-Semites were already stirring up public opinion against the Jews. Schoenberg had encountered virulent anti-Semitism for the first time in 1922, when he had been refused admission to a hotel in Mattsee, near Salzburg. "I had to break off my first working summer in five years, leave the place where I had sought to find peace in which to work; afterward I was unable to regain any peace of mind. . . ."

Berlin, in 1926, seemed more unprejudiced than Vienna, but anti-Semitism was a contagious disease that followed him to Germany. Hitler, the Austrian agitator who had become leader of the most violent of the German political parties, swept into power in 1933 with a political program that promised "Death to the Jews!" When he and his storm troopers took over the Reich chancellery, German intellectual life was virtually snuffed out. Books were burned in public bonfires; paintings of such "degenerate" artists as Cézanne, Picasso, and van Gogh were removed from the museums; "degenerate" plays and operas were banned from the stage. Whether Jewish or "Aryan," virtually all the leading German artists and intellectuals were opposed to Hitler, and most of them fled the country before they could be sent to concentration camps for "re-education" or extermination. Schoenberg, for one, emigrated to America, where he was to die in 1951, in Los Angeles, without ever having returned to

Vienna. After the end of the war, the Viennese Senate granted him the "freedom of the city" and invited him to return, but by then he was too ill to accept the invitation.

In Austria, the rise of Hitler was watched with understandable misgivings. In 1933, increasing friction between the right wing and the Socialist party led to a bloody battle between the *Heimwehr* and the *Schutzbund* (their respective private armies) that ended with the destruction of socialist influence and the establishment of a nationalist dictatorship—a so-called Christian Federal State—under Engelbert Dollfuss, the diminutive Christian Socialist leader. Since Dollfuss was unwilling to subordinate Austrian interests to those of Hitler's Reich, he was promptly assassinated by Austrian Nazis; but firm action by his successor, Kurt Schuschnigg, prevented Hitler from taking advantage of the murder, and Austria remained independent for another four years.

Most of the emigré German intellectuals fled to France, England, or the United States, but among the writers there were many who could not tear themselves away from the German language. They went to Vienna to write for emigré magazines, hoping that the Hitler régime would somehow collapse of its own accord. Walter Mehring, a brilliant Berlin poet and satirist, explained in his memoirs why he made the mistake of going to Vienna, though he had known that "the threat of an avalanche" hung over the city.

Arthur Koestler was another young writer who found that the Vienna of the mid-1930s had

121

changed for the worse: parliamentary democracy had already been abolished by Dollfuss, and there was a nervous tension in the city that reminded Koestler of the last pre-Hitler summer in Berlin. "The old waiters in the cafés still addressed their old clients as 'Herr Doktor,' but the warm familiarity had gone; there was an undefinable estrangement and aloofness, as if everybody were holding something back."

People now watched out of the corners of their eyes to see what newspapers their neighbors were reading, and what party badges they wore in their lapel. Koestler had attended the University of Vienna, and when he visited the school he was dismayed to find that the student types he had known had been replaced by "burly louts in leather shorts and white knitted knee-stockings. With stupid and provocative stares, they trampled over the mosaic pavement of the *alma mater* in their ridiculous mountaineering attire, displaying hairy legs. White stockings and leather shorts were the unofficial uniform of the Austrian Nazis." Worse yet, the lively, flirtatious female students of an earlier day had also been replaced by a new type—"the dowdy, blowsy, sweaty, pigtailed Gretchen." The pigtails, too, were a political badge. The results were a foregone conclusion: as soon as Hitler's war machine had reached the point where he could feel safe from reprisal he would add Austria to the string of "German" territories he had begun annexing to the Third Reich.

The aging Dr. Freud was still hard at work in the Berggasse—though in 1936, for fear of offending the Nazis, Viennese newspapers were not permitted to mention the fact that he was being honored on his eightieth birthday by, among others, some two hundred writers and artists headed by Thomas Mann, H. G. Wells, Romain Rolland, and Virginia Woolf. In Berlin, meanwhile, Freud's books had been ceremonially burned in a bonfire in front of the Opera House. Freud received the news with his customary equanimity. "What progress we are making!" he told his friends. "In the Middle Ages they would have burnt me; nowadays they are content with burning my books." As yet he was still confident that "the nation that produced Goethe could not possibly go to the bad," and hence was unable to foresee the time when the book burners would also turn to mass murder. Later, all of Freud's four sisters were to perish in the Holocaust.

When German troops marched into Austria on March 12, 1938, it was not only the louts in leather shorts and the girls in pigtails who were on hand to greet them. The streets of Vienna were lined with cheering crowds giving the Hitler salute. The *Führer* himself arrived in the city two days later to an ecstatic reception. On the 15th he addressed a crowd of hundreds of thousands from the balcony of the Hofburg, proclaiming a "new mission" for Austria—"the oldest eastern province of the German people shall henceforth serve as the youngest bulwark of the German Reich." In subsequent speeches he did not neglect to remind his listeners that he had "come home" to his native Austria: "I believe that it was God's will to send a youth from here into the Reich, to let him grow up, to

Just before the annexation of Austria by Hitler in 1938—and to circumvent Austrian chancellor Kurt von Schuschnigg's proposal to hold a plebiscite—the Fuehrer's men suddenly inundated Vienna with blood-red swastikas and posters like the one raised in front of St. Stephen's Cathedral (left), boldly inscribed Das Deutsche JA—*"Germany YES." Among the few Austrian writers of talent to stay behind after the Anschluss was the Viennese-born lyric poet Joseph Weinheber (right). Deeply in love with the city's half-rural suburbs, its parks, and the Wienerwald, he wrote throat-catching verses about "Old Vienna" that earned him honorary titles and prizes from the Nazis. But before the end of the war he became completely disillusioned, and in 1945, at the age of fifty-three, Weinheber committed suicide.*

raise him to be the leader of the nation so as to enable him to lead back his homeland into the Reich." A plebiscite staged by the Nazis in April produced a vote of 99.73 percent in favor of the *Anschluss,* or annexation. Even the name Austria was abolished; henceforth it was degraded to the status of the *Ostmark* ("Eastern March"), a name borrowed from Charlemagne.

From the day the Nazis marched in, Vienna became notorious for its treatment of the Jews, who then constituted about nine percent of the population. Storm troopers and SS men indulged in an orgy of sadism and looting. Many of their victims committed suicide or were sent to a huge concentration camp, Mauthausen, which was quickly set up on the north bank of the Danube. By the spring of 1941, less than 10,000 of the nearly 200,000 Viennese Jews remained in the city; about half of them had managed to escape before the outbreak of World War II; the rest were annihilated in the Nazi death factories. Dr. Freud was one of the fortunate few who were permitted to emigrate to England, thanks to the timely intervention of Marie Bonaparte, a princess of Greece and Denmark, who paid the Nazis a ransom of 250,000 Austrian schillings for his release. Before his departure, the Gestapo insisted he sign a certificate declaring he had been well treated by the secret police. Freud complied, but in a last display of his wry Viennese humor, he could not resist adding a postscript to the form letter, which he couched in the best advertising-copywriter style: "I can heartily recommend the Gestapo to anyone."

Freud had always professed a certain dislike for Vienna, but he had never seriously considered moving. Only when he reached London did he allow himself to admit his true feelings for the city which had been his home: "The feeling of triumph at being freed is too strongly mingled with grief, for in spite of everything I still greatly loved the prison from which I have been released." It was in London that he died, in September 1939, little more than a year after his escape from Vienna.

Together with Freud, Vienna lost virtually all of the intellectuals, Christian as well as Jewish, who had upheld its reputation as a center of European culture. Robert Musil escaped to Switzerland, Stefan Zweig and Oskar Kokoschka to England, Joseph Roth to France, Hermann Broch, Franz Werfel, and Ernst Krenek to the United States. Of those who were forced to remain, many perished in the concentration camps. Others, like the artist-novelist Albert Paris Gütersloh and the composer Anton von Webern, were prohibited from exercising their profession by *Berufsverbot* and could continue working only in secret, in what came to be called the "inner emigration." The only other Viennese composer of any significance to remain in the city was the elderly Franz Lehár, author of *The Merry Widow* and a dozen other successful operettas. His two Jewish librettists, Fritz Löhner and Fritz Grünbaum, were murdered in the camps, but their works continued to be performed on Viennese stages—with their names omitted from the program.

The only important literary figure to collaborate with the Nazis was Joseph Weinheber, a gifted lyric

The scope of Hitler's spectacularly staged propaganda coup is revealed in the press photograph below, taken on March 14, 1938, the day of his triumphal entry into Vienna. Standing like a conqueror in his open Mercedes, the Fuehrer leads a procession to the Rathaus, seat of the municipal government. The stately Burgtheater, symbol of Austria's devotion to the arts, is draped in swastikas and provides a theatrical backdrop for the scene. The view at right of the Albertina Platz, looking toward the Hofburg and dated October 16, 1945, shows the extensive bombing sustained by Vienna in World War II. Among the major buildings severely damaged were the Opera, St. Stephen's Cathedral, and the Belvedere—all of which have been restored.

poet who had visions of himself as the "national poet of Austria." The Nazis saw to it that he received the honorary titles and degrees he had always coveted. In exchange, he wrote verses in honor of the *Führer* and gave a few propaganda speeches. "We are the voice of the *Volk* but it is also the gods who speak through our lips," he told the party faithful at the *Grossdeutsches Dichtertreffen* (Greater-German Poetry Meeting) held at Weimar in 1938. "Today we know once again why poets and poetry exist. The *Volk* calls. . . . Dignity, Courage, Nobility, Sacrifice; it is up to us to carry these great words convincingly to the People!"

He was given the "Mozart Prize" which enabled him to buy a house in the country. Yet after a few years of Nazi-sponsored eminence he became thoroughly disillusioned with the Reich. For one thing he was poet enough to realize that Nazism had sponsored an utterly worthless "literature" created by pious hacks "who write their names in the sky with goddamned flourishes and much noise. . . . a terrible circle of mediocrities." A native of Vienna, he also resented the fact that the city's special character was being systematically destroyed, and that the *Anschluss* had deprived Austria of its individuality. Toward the end of the war, in a lecture to the students of the University of Vienna, he made a veiled confession that "in my personal life it has not always been possible for me to resist and remain true to myself—indeed I have committed actions that are not justifiable, at least to my conscience." It seemed to him that "fame has a devilish underside." Even the country house he loved had be-

come a burden on his conscience: "And what if lightning should strike the house, what then? He cannot even sell his paradise; he has invested too much in it, even his heart. This burden—he must carry it to the end. There you have it—*such* is fame." On April 8, 1945, as the Russian army fought its way into Vienna, the fifty-three-year-old Weinheber committed suicide by taking an overdose of sleeping tablets.

Many other Viennese who had welcomed the Nazis with upraised arms had changed their minds about them well before the Russians appeared at the gates. The first illegal antiwar leaflets appeared in Vienna in 1941, much to the annoyance of the Security Service of the SS. The following year the Nazi governor of Austria, Baldur von Schirach, tried to lend a certain gloss to the wartime grimness of Vienna by staging a "European Youth Festival" in the city. Representatives of Nazi-sponsored youth movements in thirteen puppet nations demonstrated their support for the Reich in a series of banquets, ceremonies, and parades. They happened to coincide with the beginnings of Hitler's defeat at Stalingrad, and the Viennese had, by then, regained some of their traditional sense of humor. "Baldur's *Kinderfest*" (children's party) became the butt of a series of underground jokes.

By March 1943, according to an SS report on home-front morale, at Viennese movie theaters "forty percent of the audience will leave the theater after the main feature without waiting to watch the newsreel." The weekly movie newsreel, distributed throughout the Reich, was one of the main vehicles

of Nazi propaganda; those who would not stay to watch it were mortally tired of Nazism and wanted no more of its broken promises. But if the Viennese had grown to dislike Hitler, the feeling was heartily reciprocated. After his triumphal *Anschluss* speeches Hitler paid only one other significant visit to the city—to sign a pact with Yugoslavia that was promptly nullified by Yugoslav rebels. The *Führer* seems to have had only suspicion and distrust toward the people of this city where he spent "five years of hardship and misery" before World War I. At the Nuremberg trials, Baldur von Schirach recalled that in 1943, Hitler spoke to him "with incredible and limitless hatred . . . against the people of Vienna." He told Schirach that "Vienna should never have been admitted into the Union of the Greater Germany," and the self-important Gauleiter came away a chastened and a sadder man. "Hitler never loved Vienna. He hated its people."

The end of Hitler's war came more quickly than anyone had foreseen. The Russian armies moved toward Vienna along the same lines of approach that had previously served the Turks and Tartars. They occupied the city on April 13, 1945; two days later, in his last general order to the troops of the Reich, Hitler declared that "Vienna will once again be German." In this, as in so many other statements, he was demonstrably wrong. When the smoke lifted, a fifth of the city lay in ruins, no one could remember ever having been pro-Nazi, and Austria reappeared on the map of Europe, its capital under four-power occupation. Nine-tenths of the people who had created its *genius loci* were dead or in exile.

On April 27, 1945, two weeks after the battle for Vienna had come to an end, the non-Nazi parties of Austria formed a provisional government under Dr. Karl Renner, who had been chancellor from 1918 to 1920, and president of the last elected Parliament, suspended by Dollfuss in 1933. The new government's first declaration read, in part: "The Republic of Austria is re-established and shall be conducted in the spirit of the constitution of 1920. The *Anschluss* imposed on the people of Austria in 1938 is null and void." In theory at least, postwar Austria was a "liberated" not an "occupied" country like Germany, and henceforth young Austrians (those who had been too young to judge the *Anschluss* for themselves) were taught at school that their country had been the "first victim of Hitler." Meanwhile, Austria was divided into four zones of Allied occupation, as was the city of Vienna. Each Allied power controlled one sector, while the inner city was under joint quadripartite control, policed by "Four in a Jeep" for the next ten years.

Many of the city's most famous landmarks lay in ruins. The State Opera had been burned out in an air raid; St. Stephen's Cathedral and the Prater had been set afire by fanatical last-ditch Nazi groups, wreaking vengeance on the "faithless" Viennese. Little of the cathedral was left standing after the fire except the outer walls and the west front, yet the great tower had stood firm and resisted the flames. The city's population had been reduced by half and now stood at less than one million. Food was so scarce that at one point the daily ration dwindled to 800 calories per person.

Ernst Fuchs' 8½-foot-high heroic bronze, The Great Queen Esther, *stands in front of his house in Vienna to commemorate the final delivery of the Jews from the Nazi holocaust of World War II. This fabulous interpretation of the Old Testament heroine who, as consort of the Persian king Ahasuerus, saved the Jewish people from annihilation, is also reminiscent of the prehistoric Great Mother, worshiped in perpetuation of the human race. Fuchs, a leading painter of the Viennese school of Fantastic Realists, is known for his apocalyptic visions of pagan and Hebraic mythology.*

Of course, food that was otherwise unavailable could always be obtained on the black market—but only by those who had something to barter in exchange. The Karlsplatz was regularly thronged with people trading jewelry, watches, clothing, and family heirlooms for small packages of meat, butter, sugar, and flour. Many of the buyers were members of the old Viennese aristocracy; poor people no longer had anything left to barter. It was the sinister age of illicit dealing in contraband goods and services that Carroll Reed depicted so brilliantly in *The Third Man.*

Gradually, however, Austria's economy returned to normal, thanks in large measure to a billion dollars in Marshall Plan aid. In 1955, after a decade of four-power "liberation," the Soviet Union, the United States, Britain, and France signed the State Treaty that gave Austria back its independence and, at the same time, committed it to a permanent policy of neutrality. In the future, Austria was to refrain from joining any of the big power blocs, and to function as a sort of second Switzerland. All the more reason, then, for Vienna to concentrate on some of the things it had traditionally known how to do best—music and art, opera and theater, publishing and tourism. Yet for a time the city's cultural life hung in the balance.

World War I had impoverished the Viennese arts; World War II had almost entirely destroyed them. To take only one typical example—of the one thousand private string quartets for which Vienna was noted before the war, less than a dozen were left to play in 1945. The Vienna Philharmonic was still

in existence, however; it had given its first "post-war" concert on April 27, 1945, while the war was still in its last throes. The singers and orchestra of the State Opera, too, began life over again—in temporary quarters in the small Theater an der Wien, which they inaugurated with a performance of *Fidelio* on October 6, 1945. (It was in this same theatre that *Fidelio* had received its world première on November 20, 1805, with Beethoven himself presiding at the pianoforte and directing the performance.) Yet such art and music as Vienna managed to produce was still oriented toward the distant past; its theaters and concert halls had become museums for the performance of bygone glories. There was no sign of a living Beethoven, Klimt, or Musil who might have had something significant to say about the contemporary state of the world.

Then, quite unexpectedly, a group of talented young men began to create a new Viennese culture out of the ashes of the old. Most of them were still in their early twenties, and they met in the Art-Club of Vienna, founded in 1946, which had its headquarters in the *Strohkoffer,* a nightclub in the basement of the Kärntner Bar. The writer Wieland Schmied recalled that, in 1949,

Hundertwasser came and told us of his journeys to Morocco and Tunis, and started controversies and discussions. Wolfgang Hutter came nearly every evening; his youthful head had already turned gray; he was always surrounded by beautiful women. Sometimes one saw Ernst Fuchs, the most restless of them all . . . with a group of pupils and disciples

to whom, like an Old-Testament prophet, he would reveal the breadth of his knowledge—that is, when he was not dancing. I have never seen anyone dance like Ernst Fuchs. And the quiet Anton Lehmden, who liked to stay in the background, though he was never overlooked. More rarely one saw Rudolf Hausner . . . and equally rarely, Albert Paris Gütersloh, the secret emperor of the Art-Club.

These were the young painters of the *Wiener Schule,* most of them now known as the "Fantastic Realists." Theirs was to become one of the few postwar movements that could hold its own against the pervasive influence of the "New York School" and the various fashionable varieties of Action Painting, Tachism, and Op or Pop art. Most of the *Wiener Schule* were, in a very real sense, survivors who had come through the war deeply scarred by their personal experiences. Rudolf Hausner, the eldest, had seen his student work banned as "degenerate" by the Nazis before being drafted into the army. Erich Brauer, the youngest, had been a slave laborer in an SS camp as a teenager. Ernst Fuchs, who became the group's spiritual leader, was also a *Mischling* (the Nazi term for a child of mixed parentage) who had been hounded from place to place as his mother tried to protect him from persecution. Friedrich Hundertwasser was also the product of a wartime tragedy: he was born with his Czech Christian father's surname, Stowasser, and served as a Hitler Youth during the same year that sixty-nine of his Jewish mother's relatives were annihilated in the camps.

Four of the five founders of the *Wiener Schule*—Lehdem, Hutter, Brauer, and Fuchs—had studied with Gütersloh at the Vienna Academy, where he had been appointed to a professorship after emerging from his "inner emigration." It was Gütersloh who taught them to explore the inner recesses of the psyche and oriented them toward dream landscapes; certainly they also learned a good deal from their nearly forgotten fellow Viennese, Dr. Freud. Their early years had been traumatized by the Nazis; as adult artists they had a great deal to say about the state of the world that could not be expressed in the Abstract Expressionism then in vogue. Out of this inner necessity they created a new and penetrating Surrealism that was closer to Hieronymous Bosch than to Salvador Dali—a "Fantastic Realism" that is at its most startling in the work of Fuchs, now a professor at the Academy and the best-known member of the *Schule.*

Born in Vienna in 1930, Ernst Fuchs revealed his precocious talent when he was a very young boy. Though his mother hid him from the Gestapo, his childhood experiences helped form his "Apocalyptic" view of the world. "Demons, devils, angels, Madonnas—right from the beginning these were the themes that fascinated me, and which I set out to paint," he explains. "But in order to make myself understood, and so that my images could be comprehended, I had to go back to the pictorial and technical methods of the old masters. And I had to discover them for myself. There was no one who taught me, for example, how to prepare a wood panel for an oil and tempera painting the way the

Ernst Fuchs (left), born in 1930 and only eight years old when Hitler took over Austria, is the youngest of the founding members of the Vienna School of Fantastic Realism. The privations of the war years, coupled with the political isolation of Vienna in the following years, fostered Fuch's visionary perception of reality deriving directly from intense personal experiences that is the hallmark of his work. In diametric opposition to the prevailing drift toward abstraction in Paris and New York, Fuchs has been obsessed with the precisionist techniques of the fifteenth-century Flemish and German masters, the better—he claims—to render with the utmost clarity the archetypal world of the imagination. The portrait of his wife, Eva Christina (below right), was intended as an icon transfiguring earthly love.

old masters did." The result, in his surrealist pictures as well as his representational nudes and portraits, was a level of traditionalist craftsmanship attained by few other modern painters.

Fuchs's vision is sometimes Gothic and occasionally Futurist. He claims to have actually seen, as well as painted, cherubs rising out of the sea and unicorns laying their heads in a virgin's lap. "Sometimes I do not understand my own images," he admits. "Only a few years later can I understand what it is that I have shown." One of the pictures he painted as an altarpiece for a Vienna church created a scandal because the figure of the crucified Christ was wearing a papal tiara. The public prosecutor brought formal charges against him because it was suspected that this was some sort of covert attack on the Catholic church. Fuchs had intended nothing of the sort; as a matter of fact, he is an intensely pious Catholic who went to a great deal of trouble to obtain a canonical annulment of his first marriage so that he could be married in church to his statuesque wife, Eva Christina, the most strikingly beautiful of all the women he has painted. Fuchs himself looks even more like an Old-Testament prophet than his well-known *Self-Portrait in a Bishop's Hat* would suggest. His beard is full and flowing; his hair has not been cut since he was seventeen and reaches nearly to his waist.

During the years following the war there was no public for an artistic style so utterly removed from both abstraction and conventional realism. Like others of the *Schule* Fuchs was happy enough to eke out a garret living as an itinerant painter. With

In contrast to some great metropolises, Vienna has never lost a close bond with nature. Surrounded as it is by the Wienerwald to the west, the Kahlenberg heights to the north, the vast open spaces of the Prater to the east, and the immense park of Schoenbrunn to the south, Vienna affords its citizens easy access to its bucolic environs. Within the city limits are formal gardens like those of the Belvedere and Schwarzenberg palaces, as well as Schoenbrunn with its tunneled allées (right)—all legacies of the Baroque era. In the very center of the city is the venerable Burggarten, with its pools of water, statues and planted vistas (left and below), once a special retreat of the imperial family.

time, however, critics and art collectors have developed a new respect for pictures bearing a recognizable resemblance to their subject matter, and the Viennese now regard Fuchs as their chief claim to fame in the world of modern art. He is the owner of a splendid fin-de-siècle mansion where he has built up a superb collection of his own and other painters' pictures—and where he also maintains a small fleet of the Rolls Royce cars.

The new Vienna also prides itself on its restored and resplendent *Staatsoper,* "the most expensive entertainment in the world," as they like to call it. Though they were far from affluent, the city fathers of postwar Vienna somehow managed to find the funds to have the old imperial opera house faithfully reconstructed, stone for stone. When the building was finally ready to open its doors to the public, in 1955, the gala first night was nothing less than a mass consecration. Thousands who could not fit into the fabulous auditorium stood outside in the drizzling rain, following a radio simulcast of the performance with their own scores, often with tears in their eyes. The opera, once again, was *Fidelio,* which has become the symbol of the city's staunch endurance in the face of adversity and conquest.

Since then, under a succession of socialist governments, the Opera's subsidies have been far larger than they ever were under the Habsburgs, who ran the institution on very moderate budgets. Not only the subsidies but also the Opera's significance and prestige are greater than ever. What happens at the *Staatsoper* is so important to Austrian musicians that the conductor (and former director)

Clemens Krauss collapsed and died of a heart attack when he learned that not he but the conductor Karl Böhm was to become music director of the resurrected opera house. Indeed, the Opera's policies are often more furiously fought over in the press than are Austrian politics, for there is no other operatic institution in the German-speaking world that can hold a candelabrum to Vienna.

In terms of international relations, Vienna has become a sort of German-speaking Geneva, particularly since the completion of its shining new United Nations City, an office complex designed to provide space for 4,500 members of the U.N. staff. In this, as in the arts and sciences, Vienna continues to fulfill its ancient role as a meeting ground for North and South, East and West. With its great architectural monuments to a vanished imperial glory, it has reemerged as a place to conduct international dialogues, to see art in the city of Klimt, to hear music in the halls where Beethoven used to play, and to partake of what is once again one of the "wonders of man." Looking down today from the tower of St. Stephen's, the cityscape has changed, but Adalbert Stifter's thoughts of 1841 have lost none of their relevance:

> Each of them and all together, in deed and thought, determines the face of the century, of the millennium—no one of them has performed this deed, but all of them together, even those who only stood by and expressed their astonishment. . . . The people build on, tirelessly, and if one falls, another is ready with hammer and trowel to take his place.

VIENNA IN LITERATURE

The Habsburg tradition of marrying rather than going to war is demonstrated in this revealing letter dated 1511 from Maximilian I to his daughter, Margaret of Austria, the politically shrewd Regent of the Netherlands, to whose guardianship were entrusted four of Maximilian's grandchildren. The letter contains a proposal for Maximilian's heir, the future Charles V, then only eleven, to marry Renée, daughter of the French king Louis XII—which never materialized—and for Ferdinand, then eight and himself to become emperor, to be betrothed to a daughter of the king of Hungary and Bohemia, a union which was sealed by treaty in 1515, through which those kingdoms became part of the Habsburg empire. The mysterious "sister of the king of England" here spoken of as a possible choice for Maximilian—who had just lost his second wife—must be Mary, the sister of Henry VIII, newly acceded to the throne of England.

IMPERIAL MARRIAGE MARKET

My dear daughter. Through my conversations with monsieur de Berttesi about getting married again, if I were so inclined, I have heard of your commission to him to tell me that in any case you favor my not doing anything that would adversely affect our grandson, the archduke Charles. I gave him my answer and also had further conversations with him about many matters, as you will hear from him.

In the first place, our talks were chiefly about the kingdom of Naples; secondly, how the king of Aragon has tried to drive the king of France and myself out of Italy; and thirdly how the king of Aragon wishes to protect the Venetians against the king of Hungary and of the fears he has that if the king of Hungary invades the kingdom of Dalmatia, then the two of us will be too close neighbors and will be in a position to drive the bastard of Aragon, as king of Naples, out of said kingdom; and fourthly we discussed how the king of Aragon spoke ill of and yet consented to the marriages of our offsprings [Ferdinand and his sister Mary] with the sole heirs of the kingdoms of Hungary, Bohemia, Moravia, Dalmatia, etc.; in the fifth place we discussed how to bring about the marriage of Reneura [Renée], second daughter of the king of France [Louis XII] and my grandson Charles; and after that, of the sister . . . of the king of England [Henry VIII] and myself. Otherwise, for the death of me, I will not marry for any amount of money, nor for any beauty. Sixthly, how as soon as peace is finally made in Italy and also in Gederland [the Netherlands], it is my desire and wish again this year to go with the king of Aragon's army against the Moors or Saracens, as the king of Aragon has requested us to, as also the king of France. In the seventh place, we talked about how the Turkish emperor wants to be my good friend, and the great battles and losses the Turks or Mahomedans have suffered against the king of Sofy [sic] both on the sea and in land encounters. . . .

Of all these many things which we talked about, my daughter, I pray that I may have in due course your sound counsel, and at the same time that you will be able to bring about the investiture of the pope against the interest of the bastard of Aragon and a pledge of the kingdom of Naples for our children, beginning with Charles, the future king of Castille, and with that all possible alliances. And so too may God have you in his holy safe-keeping.

MAXIMILIAN I
Letter to his daughter, 1511

SEAL OF VICTORY

As the capital of the Holy Roman Empire, Vienna was the citadel of the Christian West at the time of the Turkish siege of 1683. Emperor Leopold I and his court fled, entrusting the city's defense to Ernst Rüdiger Starhemberg, commandant of the City Guard. With vastly inferior manpower available and the Turks beginning to breach the fortifications, Starhemberg held out until the arrival of imperial reinforcements. The open letter from Pope Innocent XI to Starhemberg, published immediately after the rout of the Turkish armies, reflects the importance with which the event was regarded.

Beloved Son, noble Sir, Our greetings and apostolic blessing!

The indomitable steadfastness and fortitude with which you succeeded in defending the city of Vienna against the massive attacks of the mighty foe have earned you such illustrious merit in the eyes of all believers, whose safety was at stake during the siege, that the greatest honor and glory shines on your noble name wherever the Christian religion flourishes. But because this great victory which your fortitude won for the Christian world concerns Us above all, We consider it highly appropriate for Our office to extol your accomplishment through the testimony of this letter. We shall overlook no opportunity which may present itself to demonstrate under what deep obligation We are for your exploit on behalf of the Christian commonweal. May you then, intrepid man, find complete satisfaction in the exulting joy of the nations, and recognize therein the priceless fruit of your unceasing efforts; whilst We, noble Sir, are pleased to bestow upon you Our apostolic blessing as a mark of our everlasting goodwill.

POPE INNOCENT XI
Letter to Ernst Rüdiger Starhemberg, 1683

TASTE FOR MAGNIFICENCE

The dazzling life of the imperial court in Vienna at the beginning of the eighteenth century is recorded with unsparing wit and vivacity in the letters of Lady Mary Wortley Montagu during her brief stay there in the winter of 1716–1717, on her way to Constantinople, where her husband had been appointed the English ambassador. The aristocratic Lady Mary was in position to observe her Austrian peers with a congenial yet astutely discriminating eye.

To Alexander Pope *14 Sept.* [1716]

Perhaps you'l laugh at me for thanking you very gravely for all the obliging concern you express for me. 'Tis certain that I may, if I please, take the fine things you say to me for wit and railery, and it may be it would be takeing them right, but I never in my Life was halfe so well dispos'd to beleive you in earnest, and that distance which makes the continuation of your Freindship improbable has very much encreas'd my Faith for it, and I find that I have (as well as the rest of my sex), whatever face I set on't, a strong disposition to believe in miracles. Don't fancy, however, that I am infected by the air of these popish Countrys, tho I have so far wander'd from the Discipline of the Church of England to have been last Sunday at the Opera, which was perform'd in the Garden of the Favorita, and I was so much pleas'd with it, I have not yet repented my seeing it. Nothing of that kind ever was more Magnificent, and I can easily beleive what I am told, that the Decorations and habits cost the Emperour £30,000 Sterling. The Stage was built over a very large Canal, and at the beginning of the 2nd Act divided into 2 parts, discovering the Water, on which there immediately came from different parts 2 fleets of little gilded vessels that gave the representation of a Naval fight. It is not easy to imagine the beauty of this Scene, which I took particular Notice of, but all the rest were perfectly fine in their kind. The story of the Opera is the Enchantments of Alcina, which gives Oppertunity for a great variety of Machines and changes of the Scenes, which are perform'd with a surprizing swiftnesse. The Theatre is so large that 'tis hard to carry the Eye to the End of it, and the Habits in the utmost magnificence to the number of 108. No house could hold such large Decorations, but the Ladys all sitting in the open air exposes them to great Inconveniencys, for there is but one canopy for the Imperial Family, and the first night it was represented, a shower of rain happening, the Opera was broke off and the company crouded away in such confusion, I was allmost squeez'd to Death.

But if their Operas are thus delightfull, their comedys are in as high a degree ridiculous. They have but one Playhouse, where I had the curiosity to go to a German Comedy, and was very glad it happen'd to be the story of Amphitrion; that subject having been allready handled by a Latin, French and English Poet, I was curious to see what an Austrian Author would make of it. I understood enough of the language to comprehend the greatest part of it, and besides I took with me a Lady that had the Goodness to explain to me every word. The way is to take a Box which holds 4 for your selfe and company. The fix'd price is a gold Ducat. I thought the House very low and dark, but I confess the comedy admirably recompens'd that deffect. I never laugh'd so much in my Life. It begun with Jupiter's falling in Love out of a peep hole in the clouds and ended with the Birth of Hercules; but what was most pleasant was the use Jupiter made of his metamorphose, for you no sooner saw him under the figure of Amphitrion, but instead of flying to Alcmena with the raptures Mr. Dryden puts into his mouth, he sends to Amphitrion's Tailor and cheats him of a lac'd Coat, and his Banker of a bag of money, a Jew of a Di'mond ring, and bespeaks a great Supper in his name; and the greatest part of the comedy turns upon poor Amphitrion's being tormented by these people for their debts, and Mercury uses Sosia in the same manner. But I could not easily pardon the Liberty the Poet has taken of Larding his play with not only indecent expressions, but such grosse Words as I don't think our Mob would suffer from a Mountebank. . . .

To Lady Mar *14 Sept.* [1716]

Tho I have so lately trouble'd you (dear Sister) with a long letter, yet I will keep my promise in giving you an Account of my first going to Court.

In order to that ceremony, I was squeez'd up in a Gown and adorn'd with a Gorget and the other implements thereunto belonging: a dresse very inconvenient, but which certainly shews the neck and shape to great advantage. I cannot forbear in this place giving you some description of the Fashions here, which are more monstrous and contrary to all common sense and reason than tis possible for you to imagine. They build certain fabricks of Gause on their heads about a yard high consisting of 3 or 4 storys fortify'd with numberless yards of heavy riband. The foundation of this structure is a thing they call a Bourlé, which is exactly of the same shape and kind, but about 4 times as big, as those rolls our prudent milk maids make use of to fix their Pails upon. This machine they cover with their own Hair, which they mix with a great deal of false, it being a particular beauty to have their heads too large to go into a moderate Tub. Their Hair is prodigiously powder'd to conceal the mixture, and set out with 3 or 4 rows of Bodkins, wonderfully large, that stick 2 or 3 inches from their Hair, made of Diamonds, Pearls, red, green and yellow stones, that it certainly requires as much art and Experience to carry the Load upright as to dance upon May Day with the Girland. Their whalebone petticoats out-do ours by several yards Circumference and cover some Acres of Ground. You may easily suppose how much this extrodinary Dresse sets off and improves the natural Uglyness with which God Allmighty has been pleas'd to endow them all generally. Even the Lovely Empresse her selfe is oblig'd to comply in some degree with these absurd Fashions, which they would not quit for all the World.

I had a private Audience (according to ceremony) of halfe an hour and then all the other Ladys were permitted to come make their Court. I was perfectly charm'd with the Empresse.

LADY MARY WORTLEY MONTAGU
Letters, 1763

SOURCES OF MUSIC

Vienna in the eighteenth century was still too far off the beaten track to be ordinarily included in the Grand Tour; but this did not deter the English musicologist Charles Burney from journeying there down the Danube, bent on collecting material for his History of Music. Arriving in the late summer of 1772, he was enormously helped by the British Ambassador Viscount Stormont, who saw to it that Burney met not only the musicians but also their wealthy patrons. Probably the most important was the Countess Maria Wilhelmina von Thun, that "light-hearted" patroness of Gluck, Haydn, and Mozart to whom Beethoven was later to dedicate one of his piano trios.

This city, the capital of the empire, and residence of the imperial family, is so remote from England, has been so imperfectly described, by writers of travels, and is so seldom visited by Englishmen, that I should have presented my readers with a minute account of its public buildings and curiosities, if it had not furnished me with ample materials for a long article, relative to my principal subject, music, to which every other must give place. . . .

The streets are rendered doubly dark and dirty by their narrowness, and by the extreme height of the houses; but, as these are chiefly of white stone, and in a uniform, elegant style of architecture, in which the Italian taste prevails, as well as in music, there is something grand and magnificent in their appearance, which is very striking; and even many of those houses which have shops on the ground floor, seem like palaces above. Indeed the whole town and its suburbs, appear, at the first glance, to be composed of palaces, rather than of common habitations. . . .

The emperor's prerogative of having the first floor of almost every house in Vienna for the use of the officers of his court and army, is as singular in itself, as it is inconvenient to the inhabitants. The houses are so large, that a single floor suffices for most of the first and largest families in the city.

The inhabitants do not, as elsewhere, go to the shops to make purchases; but the shops are *brought to them*; there was literally a fair, at the inn where I lodged, every day. The tradespeople seem to sell nothing at home, but, like hawkers and pedlars, carry their goods from house to house. A stranger is teased to death by these chapmen, who offer to sale wretched goods, ill manufactured, and ill fashioned. In old England, it is true, things are very dear, but if their goodness be compared with these, they are cheap as dirt.

I must observe, that I have never yet found, in any country on the Continent, that the tradespeople, like many in England, could be trusted, without beating them down, and fixing the price of what is purchased of them, previous to possession. In London there is little danger of being charged unreasonably for anything that is had from a reputable shop, though the price is not asked, when the goods are sent for, nor paid, till the bill is brought in, perhaps a year after. . . .

. . . This morning was spent in the imperial library and at the Countess Thun's, who was on the point of going to Laxenberg for a longer time .than I was likely to stay in Vienna. This was an afflicting circumstance, as her house was always open to me, and she did everything in her power to procure me entertainment and friends. . . .

She was now surrounded by her friends, who, though they were not in my situation, but were sure of seeing her again very soon, either here, or at Laxenberg; yet they had almost tears in their eyes, at the thoughts of losing her, only for a few days. During this visit she was so kind as to produce all her musical curiosities, for me to hear and see, before we parted. Her taste is admirable, and her execution light, neat and feminine; however, she told me that she *had* played much better than at present, and humorously added, that she had had six children, and that "every one of them had taken something from her". She is a cheerful, lively, and beneficent being, whom everyone here seems to love as a favourite sister. She is niece to the once handsome prince Lobkowitz, who was in England in 1745 and '46, and much connected with the famous count St. Germain, who made so much noise at that time, not only with his fiddle, but his mysterious conduct and equivocal character. This prince [Lobkowitz] is now retired from the world, and will not see even his relations and best friends for many months together. He had cultivated music so far, as not only to play and to judge well, but even to compose in a superior manner; and his niece gave me several of his pieces, which had great merit and novelty, particularly a song for two orchestras, which no master in Europe need be ashamed of.

. . . In the afternoon, I called on M. L'Augier, and there among other company met again with the Florentine poet Abata Casti, who repeated several of his poems, particularly a tale from Voltaire, called *L'Art d'élever une Fille*; which was extremely arch and comic.

M. L'Augier, being in the service of the court, was obliged to attend the emperor the next day at Laxenberg; I was sorry to lose him, as his house was an excellent retreat, when I could spare the time to enjoy it; and his conversation concerning music and musicians was in a particular manner entertaining and profitable.

DR. CHARLES BURNEY
Continental Travels, 1770–1772

CONCERT AND CARNIVAL

Two years after moving to Vienna from his family home in Salzburg, Wolfgang Amadeus Mozart wrote his father this letter reporting on the widening recognition his music was being accorded in the capital. Mozart's irrepressible creative activity is reflected in his account of an impromptu musical pantomime.

Vienne, *ce* 12 *de Mars,* 1783

Mon Très Cher Père!

I hope that you have not been uneasy but have guessed the cause of my silence, which was that, as I did not know for certain how long you would stay in Munich, I delayed writing until now, when I am almost sure that my letter will find you in Salzburg. My sister-in-law, Madame Lange, gave her concert yesterday in the theatre and I played a concerto. The theatre was very full and I was received again by the Viennese public so cordially that I really ought to feel delighted. I had already left the platform, but the audience would not stop clapping and so I had to repeat the rondo; upon which there was a regular torrent of applause. It is a good advertisement for my concert which I am giving on Sunday, March 23rd. I added my symphony which I composed for the Concert Spirituel. My sister-in-law sang the aria "Non so d'onde viene". Gluck had a box beside the Langes, in which my wife was sitting. He was loud in his praises of the symphony and the aria and invited us all four to lunch with him next Sunday. It is possible that the German opera may be continued, but no one knows what will happen. One thing is certain, and that is, that Fischer is off to Paris in a week. I entreat you most earnestly to send me the oboe concerto I gave to Ramm—and as soon as possible. When doing so, you might put in something else, for example, the original scores of my masses and of my two vesper compositions. This is solely with a view to Baron van Swieten [prefect of the court library] hearing them. He sings treble, I sing alto (and play at the same time), Starzer sings tenor and young Teiber from Italy sings bass. Send me in the meantime the "Tres sunt" by Haydn, which will do until you can let me have something else of his. Indeed I should very much like them to hear the "Lauda Sion". The full score of the "Tres sunt" copied out *in my own handwriting* must be somewhere at home. The fugue "In te Domine speravi" has won great applause and so have the "Ave Maria" and the "Tenebrae" and so forth. I beg you to enliven our Sunday music practices with something soon.

On Carnival Monday our company of masqueraders went to the Redoute, where we performed a pantomime which exactly filled the half hour when there is a pause in the dancing. My sister-in-law was Columbine, I Harlequin, my brother-in-law Pierrot, an old dancing master (Merk) Pantaloon, and a painter (Grassi) the doctor. Both the plot and the music of the pantomime were mine. Merk, the dancing master, was so kind as to coach us, and I must say that we played it charmingly. I am enclosing the programme which was distributed to the company by a mask, dressed as a postillion. The verses, although only doggerel, might have been done better. I had nothing to do with them. Müller, the actor, dashed them off. Well, I must close, for I am going to a concert at Count Esterhazy's. Meanwhile farewell. Please do not forget about the music. My wife and I kiss your hands a thousand times and embrace our dear sister with all our hearts and I am ever your most obedient son.

WOLFGANG AMADEUS MOZART
Letter to his father, 1783

After Napoleon's defeat, his marriage to the archduchess Marie Louise created an ambiguous situation in the Habsburg court which is reflected in this description of a visit to Schoenbrunn in 1814 by the Comte Auguste de La Garde, in the company of the widely traveled Belgian aristocrat, Prince Charles Joseph de Ligne. It was at Schoenbrunn that Napoleon's son, the Prince of Parma, was sequestered when Napoleon was sent to Elba. The young prince, then four years old, was placed in the care of a French lady, Mme. de Montesquiou, under the watchful eye of his grandfather, the emperor Francis I, whose aim it was to bring him up as an Austrian prince.

A PRINCELY VISIT

Schönbrunn, the building of which was begun by the princes of the House of Austria, was the object of Maria-Theresa's particular affection. It was she who completed it, and, in order to accelerate the work, part of it was done by torchlight. The castle is delightfully situated on the right bank of the Wien. The majestic *ensemble* of its architecture proclaims it at once to be a royal residence. The gardens, nobly and most gracefully planned, interspersed with sheets of limpid water skilfully disposed, planted with trees of the most luxuriant vegetation, and studded with most precious marble and bronze statuary, harmonise most imposingly with the magnificence of the palace itself. The park is alive with deer of all kinds, the peaceful tenants of those beautiful spots, and they, as it were, seem to invite the approach of the visitors. Every day and at all hours these glades and avenues are open to the public. Numberless carriages and horsemen are constantly there. The park is surrounded by pleasaunces, the inmates of which in the milder season are the eyewitnesses of a succession of fêtes and rejoicings. The sound of those rejoicings pierces the walls of the imperial habitation, and adds by its animation to the charms of the noble pile.

The apartments of the palace are spacious and furnished with exquisite taste. There are several rooms entirely draped with black: they have remained in that condition since the death of Maria-Theresa's husband. A small study is decorated with drawings by the various archduchesses. This is the room where Napoleon, during his sojourn at Schönbrunn,

retired to work. It is there he beheld for the first time the portrait of Marie-Louise, and perhaps conceived the idea of a union which had such an influence on his destiny.

A staircase leads from that room into the garden. On a wooded height stands a charming pavilion built by Maria-Theresa, and called 'La Gloriette'; that elegant structure of fairy-like design, composed of arcades, colonnades, and trophies, bounds the vistas and constitutes one of the most delightful pieces of decorative architecture. It is at the same time a palace and a triumphal arch. It is reached by a double staircase. The view from the principal drawing-room defies description: there are immense masses of green as far as the eye can reach, and at the horizon are the city of Vienna, the course of the Danube, and finally the high mountains whose outlines constitute the background of the magnificent landscape. It is difficult to imagine a more splendid panorama.

The greenhouses of Schönbrunn are perhaps the most beautiful in Europe. They contain precious samples of the vegetation of the universe. It was there that Emperor Francis, who had a particular liking for botanical pursuits, himself attended to the rarest plants.

Not far from there is the zoological collection, disposed in a circle around a pavilion forming the centre, as it were, of the various sheltered enclosures for the animals. Each species has its *habitat* and its garden, with the plants and trees proper to the country of its birth. There, though prisoners, the animals apparently enjoy their liberty.

Close to the castle there was a small railed-off plot, carefully tended, which was the garden of the son of Napoleon. It was there that the young prince cultivated the flowers which each morning he gathered into bouquets for his mother and his governess.

While crossing the courts, which are very spacious, the prince pointed out the spot where, while Napoleon was inspecting some troops, a young fanatic attempted to kill him about the time of the battle of Wagram. If a crime of that nature is calculated to inspire anything but a feeling of indignation, that young fellow might have been pitied in virtue of the courage and fortitude he showed at the moment of his death.

It was in those courts that, at the same period, Napoleon gave orders to his ordnance-officer, the Prince de Salm, to put through its drill a regiment of the Germanic Confederation, and to give the command in German. The Viennese came down in shoals, this little amenity on the part of the victor having made them forget that their capital was in the hands of the enemy.

In the hall a French servant, still wearing the Napoleonic livery, came towards us. He knew the marshal, and immediately went to inform Mme. de Montesquiou of his arrival.

'I trust we'll not have to wait,' said my companion, 'for, as I have told you, I am almost like the Comte de Ségur of Schönbrunn.' He alluded to the position of grand-master of the ceremonies that nobleman, whom he had known at the Court of Catherine, had occupied near the person of Napoleon.

A few moments later Mme. de Montesquiou came to apologise for being unable to introduce us immediately. 'The little prince,' she said, 'is sitting for his portrait to Isabey, which is intended for the Empress Marie-Louise. As he is very fond of the marshal, the sight of him would only make him restless. I'll see that the sitting is as short as possible.'

'You know what happened at my first visit?' remarked the prince, after Mme. de Montesquiou had left us. 'When they told the child that Marshal Prince de Ligne had come to see him, he exclaimed: "Is it one of the marshals who deserted papa? Don't let him come in." They had a good deal of trouble in making him understand that France is not the only country where they have marshals.'

A short while afterwards Mme. de Montesquiou took us to the apartments. When young Napoleon caught sight of the Prince de Ligne he slid off his chair, and flung himself into the arms of the old soldier. He was indeed as handsome a child as one could wish to see, and the likeness to his ancestress Maria-Theresa was positively striking. The cherub-like shape of his face, the dazzling whiteness of the skin, the eyes full of fire, and the pretty fair curls drooping on his shoulders, made up one of the most graceful models ever offered to Isabey. He was dressed in a richly embroidered uniform of hussars, and wore on his dolman the star of the Legion of Honour. '*Bon jour, monsieur,*' said the little lad, 'I like the French very much.'

Remembering the words of Rousseau to the effect that people do not like to be questioned, and least of all children, I stooped down and kissed him.

COMTE AUGUSTE DE LA GARDE-CHAMBONAS
Journal of a Nobleman, 1833

The distinguished nineteenth-century English physician Richard Bright (1789–1859) happened to be in Vienna attending the highly reputed Vienna School of Medicine when the Congress of Vienna convened. With the habit of incisive observation for which he was known, Bright recorded—not without humor—his impressions of that unprecedented fraternal gathering of emperors, kings, and ambassadors from every corner of Europe.

IN ROYAL COMPANY

It was Sunday; the shops were all closed, and, in addition to the mass, which is daily and almost hourly celebrated in all the churches, sermons were preached in the German language. It is a day of more than ordinary festivity amongst all the ranks; the theatres are open in the evening; and I was strongly recommended to visit a place of public amusement called the Redoute, where, in all probability, I should see many of the distinguished persons then collected at the Congress.

Not having yet delivered my letters, I accompanied a gentleman of Vienna, with whom I had made an accidental acquaintance. We entered the room about nine o'clock in the evening. It is a magnificent saloon, finely lighted, surrounded by a gallery, and forming part of the large pile of building called the Bourg or Imperial Palace. Never was an assembly less ceremonious; every one wore his hat; many, till the room became heated, their great-coats; and no one pretended to appear in an evening dress, except a few Englishmen, who, from the habits of

our country, and some little vanity, generally attempt to distinguish themselves by an attention to outward appearances. Around the whole circumference of the room were four or five rows of benches, occupied, for the most part, by well-dressed females; while the other parts presented a moving multitude, many of whom were in masks, or in dominos, and were busily engaged in talking and laughing, or dancing to the music of a powerful orchestra. My companion squeezed my arm, as we passed a thin figure with sallow shrunken features, of mild expression, with a neck, stiff, bending a little forwards, and walking badly. "That is our Emperor." I shook my head and smiled. He was alone, and dressed like the rest. "Pray allow me to doubt a little till I have some farther proof."—"There, do you see that little man with white hair, a pale face, and aquiline nose? He was almost pushed down as he passed the corner;—that is the King of Denmark." Again I shook my head in disbelief. "Here the Emperor of Russia approaches." I looked up, and found the information true. His fine manly form, his round and smiling countenance, and his neat morning dress, were not to be mistaken; they were the same which, some months before, I had seen enter the church at Harlem, to the thundering peals of the grand organ. I soon recognized the tall form, the solemn and grave features, of the King of Prussia; and afterwards seeing these two in familiar conversation with the two monarchs, whose pretensions I had disputed, was satisfied their claims were just. "That short, thick, old gentleman, is the grand Duke of Saxe Weimar. That young man near him, the Crown Prince of Wirtemberg. Here, turn your eyes to that seat. The large elderly man, with a full face,—he looks like an Englishman,—he is the king of Bavaria."—"Pardon," I exclaimed, stepping quickly aside. "That was the grand Duke of Baaden," said my monitor, "whose toe you trod upon; he was talking to Prince William of Prussia. Here, fall back a little to let these gentlemen pass, they seem very anxious to go on. One, two, three, four, five;—these are all Archdukes of Austria.—There seems a little press towards that end of the room. See, three women in masks have beset the King of Prussia; he seems not a little puzzled what he shall do with them.—Now a party of waltzers draws the attention of the crowd, and the King is left to dispose of his fair assailants as he thinks fit. Do you see that stout tall man, who looks at the dance?—he is the Duke of Saxe Coburg; and by his side, not so stout as himself, is his brother the Prince Leopold."—"Who is this young man next to us, marked with the small-pox, who is speaking broken English?" "It is the Crown Prince of Bavaria; he is said to be very fond of your nation. And here," giving me another hearty squeeze with his elbow, "is an English milord." He had on his head a remarkably flat cocked hat,—two ladies in dominos leaned upon his arm. The hat, unique of its kind, rather excited a smile in my companion. After a little more pushing, for the room was now become very full, we encountered a fine dark military looking man, not in uniform of course, but with mustachoes. "This was Beauharnois, viceroy of Italy." In this way, for two or three hours, did we continue meeting and pushing amongst hundreds of men, each of whom, had he but made his appearance singly at a fashionable rout in London, would have furnished a paragraph to our newspapers, prints to our shops, titles to our bazaars, distinctive appellations to every article of our dress, and themes, if not ideas, to our poets.

RICHARD BRIGHT, M.D.
Travels from Vienna Through Lower Hungary, 1818

The celebrated Order of the Golden Fleece, the exclusive confraternity of knighthood founded in 1429 by Philip the Good of Burgundy, was comprised of noblemen who swore to defend the Christian faith and remain loyal to their sovereign. In 1478, upon Maximilian's marriage to Philip's granddaughter, Mary of Burgundy, he became Grand Master of the Order, with the prerogative to choose its thirty-one knights. From then on the Golden Fleece remained in Habsburg hands: first, in Spain; then, following the death of Philip II, the order was moved with great ceremony by the emperor Charles VI to Vienna. The ceremonial installation of new knights is described in the following passage from Vienna and the Austrians, *by Frances Trollope, author of travel books and mother of the novelist Anthony Trollope.*

HABSBURG CEREMONY

30th November, 1836

We have this morning witnessed by far the most splendid pageant I ever saw,—namely, the installation of eleven knights of the order of the Golden Fleece. The Archduke Albert, and his brother the Archduke Charles, sons of the renowned Archduke Charles, who is uncle to the Emperor, were among them; and the ceremony being altogether one of great dignity and parade, the demand for tickets was very urgent: but, by the kindness of Prince Metternich and Sir Frederic Lamb, we all obtained places; and Mr. H——, as usual, contrived to make a very accurate drawing, notwithstanding the crowd.

We were directed to repair to the palace at ten o'clock, as the press in all the rooms leading to the Salle des Cérémonies was expected to be great, and there might have been difficulty in reaching our places at a later hour. On ascending the principal stairs of the palace, we found that, early as we were, a multitude of others were earlier still, for the throng was already such as to make the progress to the great hall a work of some labour. The crowd however, for the most part, consisted of the military on duty, and the different official attendants on the court. A vast number of courtiers likewise in the richest full-dress were lounging in all the rooms; and not only many who were making their way to the same tribune in the grande salle as ourselves, but many more, whose tickets admitted them only to the rooms through which the royal cortège was to pass, contributed to make the scene one of great movement and bustle.

Having at length safely reached our places, which were in a temporary gallery commanding an excellent view of the whole room, we found ample occupation for the time, before the ceremonies began, in contemplating the varied and brilliant groups of gentlemen that already occupied the floor of the hall. Through this glittering phalanx a stream of ladies were already pressing forward to the different tribunes allotted to them. There were seats in none, except those prepared for the Empress and her ladies, and a few more placed in the tribune set apart for the foreign ministers. . . . The costumes displayed upon this occasion among the gentlemen surpass, both in elegance of outline and richness of decoration, all I had expected to see; though I had heard much before-hand of the great splendour of the Hungarian nobles.

I really know nothing at once so gorgeous and picturesque as the uniform of the Hungarian noble body-guard, with their splendid silver accoutrements, their spotted furs, uncut, hanging at their backs, and their yellow morocco boots. The rich and beautiful skins which they all carry, apparently in the very shape in which they came off the animal, give a most striking air of primitive and almost barbarous magnificence.

The other, and more distinguished Hungarian nobles, wore all of them the remarkable national costume of their proud and stately country; and a finer set of men, or dresses better calculated to set their persons off to advantage, cannot easily be imagined. The military uniforms, also, are prodigiously superb; and so various, that it required very attentive study to become acquainted with them all. The multiplied and brilliant decorations of Austria are no trifling addition to the magnificence of their full-dress; and whether it were from the effect of this very effective toilet, or from their personal dignity and grace, I will not pretend to decide,—but, whatever the cause, I certainly thought that I had never looked on so elegant an assembly of men before.

The hall itself, as I think I have told you before, is a very fine room, lofty and well-proportioned, with a row of stately columns on each side of it, and decorated with abundance of mirrors and chandeliers. On this occasion the upper end of the chamber was decorated by a magnificent throne, placed on an ample richly-carpeted dais. The draperies of the canopy were of crimson velvet, heavily embroidered with gold, and terminating at each corner with enormous plumes of white feathers; so that, large and lofty as was the apartment, this splendid erection was majestically conspicuous from every corner of it. . . .

At length, a flourish of trumpets announced the approach of the court, and sent all the sabred, starred, and cordoned loiterers back in thick ranks against the galleries, leaving more space than a moment before seemed possible, for the entrance of those to look upon whom we were all assembled there.

The first person who stepped forward into the space thus cleared was the Empress of Austria, her tall and elegant figure shown to great advantage by a dress of black velvet, very richly ornamented about the front and shoulders by diamonds. A white hat and feathers, with a brilliant bandeau of diamonds under it, formed her head-dress; and a rich blond scarf, thrown over her very gracious shoulders, prevented her dress from having so completely the air of an evening toilet as it would have had without it. She walked up the room quite alone, bowing very graciously to the tribunes and to the throng of courtiers marshalled on both sides of her below them. . . . Then followed the tall and majestic Archduchess Sophia, consort of the Archduke Francis, leading her two little boys,—the eldest of them being presumptively "the hope of the fair state." Next to her came the Archduchess Clementina, Princess of Salerno, leading her fair little girl; and then the very pretty young Archduchess Maria Theresa, who in a few weeks is to become Queen of Naples.

The Prince of Salerno, and three young archdukes, followed, completing the party admitted to the tribune of the Empress. A white-plumed host of fair ladies followed, all I think in black velvet dresses. Soon after they had taken their places, another flourish of trumpets was heard from the music gallery, and three very significant taps on the floor from some official baton again cleared the way, making the crowd, which appeared quite sufficient to fill the whole, shrink into about half the space.

Then entered the Emperor, in his robes as grand master of the order, and his cortège, consisting upon this occasion wholly of knights of the Golden Fleece, each followed by an elegant young page to bear his train; and a more splendid line it would be impossible to look upon. The whole procession, including the eleven new knights, were all attired in the rich robes of the order; while their collars and caps, radiant with jewels, formed altogether as imposing a spectacle as it is possible for draperies and decorations to produce.

FRANCES TROLLOPE
Vienna and the Austrians, 1838

As the capital of a multinational empire, Vienna for centuries attracted foreigners to the ranks of its highly stratified population. Especially among the lower working classes, these foreigners remained unassimilated even into the nineteenth century, retaining the language and habits of their origins and living together in their own quarters of the city. The following account by an Austrian traveler is excerpted from a book published four years before the Revolution of 1848.

CABBAGES AND KINGS

The most celebrated of all the women of Vienna is, beyond doubt, Maria Theresa, but the most noted are the so-called "Fratschelweiber." Like their sisters in the cabbage-market of Königsberg, and the Halles of Paris, they are distinguished for their eloquence, their presence of mind, and their inexhaustible wit. It is said that the Emperor Joseph went once incognito among them, and purposely overturned a basket of eggs, in order to have a specimen of their oratorical powers. Their chief seat is in the "Hof," one of the largest squares of the city, where they deal in vegetables, fruit, cheese, and other articles of food.

What I saw and heard of these interesting persons gave me more amusement than I can hope to give the reader by a description, for when the naïve originality of the Vienna dialect comes into print, it gives no more idea of it as spoken, than the printed notes do of the sound of a piece of music.

I must confess, that often when I returned from the "Fratschel" market I used to feel as if I had been in a madhouse, so incessant and clapper-like had been the chatter about every thing in and about the world—about the *"Germnudeln"* which they were recommending to Herr *von* Nachtigall, an old hairdresser, whose poverty shone out from every side of his worn and rented nether garments, but on whom they bestowed the *"von"* nevertheless because he held a few kreuzers in hand; about the butcher, "the stingy hound, who had sold them such a miserable little bit of meat to-day." They spared neither the emperor, the pope, nor their ministers, and, least of all, the people of rank and fashion, whom they saw driving about. I was one day witness of the little ceremony used with the latter. At the corner of the "Hof," a careless coachman ran over a boy. In an instant a crowd of women and men were in full pursuit of the flying vehicle, in which sat a lady and gentleman of the higher class. But the Fratschelweiber paid not the smallest heed to their high nobility. "Catch 'em there, bring 'em back, the quality candle-snuffers! bring 'em back! the scum of a dunghill! To run over the poor boy!" were the compliments that ran from mouth to mouth, as the mob ran bawling after the gentles, who would probably have fared ill enough, if they had fallen into the hands of the irritated rabble. This class of persons in Vienna are by no means the patient, respectful, timid herd to be met with in other capitals of monarchical states; for example, in St. Petersburg, Moscow, Prague, &c. The child, whose cause was so energetically adopted by the Fratschel women, was not even a countryman, but a little Croat, such as are met with in all parts of Vienna, selling radishes and onions. Beyond a bruise or two, he had sustained no injury; indeed, he had rather been knocked down than ran over. The women put on his broad-brimmed Croatian hat again, wiped carefully his wide mantle of thick white wool, in which he looked like a diminutive Orlando in a giant's armour, and bought some of his radishes to console him. The child, who understood not a word of the Fratschel jargon, looked round him in a scared manner, and then resumed his monotonous cry, "*An guten ratti, ratti,*" (good radishes), the only German he knew. These Croats are very numerous in Vienna, and form no inconsiderable portion of the populace there. As they sell nothing but onions and radishes, the Fratschel ladies are persuaded that Croatia must be a poor country and produce nothing else. In the suburbs, there are, in the public-houses of the lowest class, great dormitories for them which they call Croat quarters. There when the ravens return from the fields to Stephan's tower, the poor Croats huddle together after the fatigues of the day, and sleep in the same thick cloaks that have sheltered them from the heat during the day. "They live like so many cattle," said one of the Fratschel women to me, "they haven't even a bedstead, let alone a mattress. They lie o' nights and holidays on their bellies, and are fit for nothing but to sell onions."

J. G. KOHL
Austria: Vienna, Prague, Hungary, Bohemia and the Danube, 1844

DAYS TO REMEMBER

This description of Vienna's famous Prater by the Austrian writer Adalbert Stifter offers a poignant vision of life in the Biedermeier period around 1840. The country was still under the political guidance of Prince Metternich, but this account indicates to what extent the people, under the benevolent rule of the emperor Ferdinand I, retained a nostalgic pride in the splendor of the Habsburg court. Stifter was also a painter, and his habit of visual observation gives a vivid pictorial quality to his writing, heightened by a certain whimsical, cozy humor which is the essence of Biedermeier.

Few great cities in the world have anything to compare with our Prater. "Is it a park?" No. "Is it a meadow?" No. "Is it a public garden?"

No. "A forest preserve?" No. "Amusement grounds?" No. "What then?" All of these put together. At the east end of Vienna there is a large island in the Danube which was originally a watery meadow like so many islands in the Danube where it flows through the flat plain, but which in the course of time has become an enchanting mixture of field and forest, park and playground, promenades for the milling crowds and walks of the utmost solitude, noisy garden cafés and quiet clearings. There may be many in Vienna who are completely unaware of the beauties of their Prater even though it is so frequented; for as deafening as the teeming throng is in some places and at certain times, elsewhere it is as lonely as a desert, so that as one wanders through these fields and woodlands one might expect more to come upon a rustic dairy than upon the palatial residence of a great monarchy. But precisely because such a palatial residence requires a gigantic garden for its populace to pour into and yet leave some parts empty enough for the lonely wanderer and observer, it is fortunate that we have the Prater. The citizen of Vienna is well enough aware of this, and even though he is at times somewhat ungrateful towards his Prater, as for example in the hot summer months, at other times he is even more passionately attached to it, as for example in the spring and particularly on special days when it is in style to drive in the Prater, or failing that, at least to walk. The first and second of May are such days, also Easter Monday and Pentecost. Now imagine such a day, far off reader, and follow me there in spirit; let this essay show you what we see.

It is the first of May, about four o'clock in the afternoon, and also a Sunday, under the brightest sky.

We pass over the Ferdinand Bridge into the suburb of Leopoldstadt and turn immediately to the right towards the Jägerzeile, which leads to the Prater; the whole of that beautiful unusually broad street is filled with a dark stream of people billowing so densely that if someone were offered a dukedom on condition that he would go the length of the street without brushing against anyone, he would never win. In the midst of this human stream go the carriages like ships in ice floes, for the most part slowly, often held up and standing still for minutes at a time; then, when the line of carriages has thinned out, flowing after one another like gleaming phantoms past the more quietly promenading crowd of spectators. Here and there projecting out of the sea of pedestrians bounce the figures of equestrians, while the generally splendid houses along this street rise up peacefully above the shoving, swirling crowds of people, their windows and balconies filled with countless spectators, there to watch the brilliant procession flowing past their eyes, and to delight in the magnificence, the shimmer and the glitter. Most of them are ladies who, in dresses of all colors, look down from the windows onto this springtime animation like blossoming shrubs. Around a quarter to four one might think that the whole city had gone mad and was now promenading with obsessive compulsion down along this street, and that you and I, dear stranger, are promenading there also.

Then at the end of the street up through the dust loom the stately trees of the Prater, towards which we all stream as if eternal salvation

were to be dispensed there. Finally the long Jägerzeile comes to an end, and various routes radiate out from one another like the points of a star, and the human mass becomes dispersed. Banners wave from high masts and direct the wanderers in various directions; the flag at our left bears on its fluttering tongue high in the air the words "Ferdinands-Nordbahn," and indeed in that direction now hasten carriages packed with people toward the left of the station, where the iron horses are already waiting and snorting, ready to pull an endless train of wagons out to the Marchfeld, or even to Brünn, which has become one of our suburbs through the speed of these steeds. The middle banner points the way to the swimming school, which happens to be celebrating its opening today. The third banner carries the name "Rador," or "Sophie," or some other, and a mighty arm points to the steamboat entrance. Further to the right there is an open lawn on which stand the wooden huts of the menagerie, where the animals represented on enormous canvases make them even more frightening than they appear in reality within. These paintings and the exotic cries and whistling and cooing and roaring inside attract the people so that there is always a dense crowd at the entrance, and in the gleeful glances of the children and country girls can be read the lively desire to see what there is inside. Out on the open lawn are also booths with fruits and baked goods, a Croatian with sponges and flints, a man on stilts, and another with a hurdy-gurdy with a dog on it who can stand on its hind legs and shoulder a sword in its paw.

But past all these things goes the human stream down the Hauptallee; for there today is to be seen the highest, the high and the lowest of the Viennese world. What only caprice and riches can contrive in the way of brilliant apparel, equipages and servants is to be seen today in the Hauptallee. On both sides are shaded pathways, one for the pedestrians, the other for the equestrians; in the middle of the principal thoroughfare drive innumerable carriages, one hard upon another, down one side and up another to avoid collisions, and this process is repeated often, in order to see and to be seen—for this is precisely the place where color vies with dazzling color, charm with charm, splendor with splendor, riches with riches, graceful movement with graceful movement, to such a degree that it is bewildering to anyone who has not seen it before.

On both sides of the main avenue stand the spectators, closely packed, and behind their backs surges the colorful stream of promenaders, while in the middle roll carriages upon carriages, a scintillating, shimmering train, well over half a mile long. Over there in a carriage which floats along as easily as an airship, a lady of the highest rank glides past, dressed in magnificent simplicity, adorned with few but costly jewels; and immediately behind her is the family of a rich burgher; and there, a carriage full of merry children who find no end to their astonishment and excitement over the splendor which surrounds them. Here comes a man standing entirely alone in his carriage parading for the first time with four matchless steeds; some riders now gallop past and greet a carriage from which the most beautiful countenance nods back. And there sits a lonely old man in his heavy coach; he is clad in fine sable and bears many tiny little crosses on his breast.

Then comes a hackney coach with jolly clerks or students—then others and again others and everything dances before your eyes as if it would never end, and out of the pomp and shimmer wells still more pomp and shimmer, and as all this drifts by and surges and gushes you stand there watching a spectacle such as only the Prater can offer.

Close by the smart crowd stands a stag, holding high his stately antlers and gloating with foolishly wise eyes at the seething crowd; it is something he has witnessed often before, but it was never quite so boisterous as today, and therefore after watching it for a moment he goes off back to his pastures; and no one is surprised, for everyone knows that the Prater belongs to stags and walkers. On and on floods the procession, and while the splendor of dress, the beauty of horses and carriages, the waving of feathers, the sparkle of jewelry dazzle your eye, yet it happens—and not seldom—that out of the multitude there emerges a face that makes you forget everything, as it glides past your eyes in its soft beauty, so that you look after it eagerly, and it often seems that you are the poorer after it has gone. But just wait, Vienna is not so poor in feminine beauty; perhaps an equal will come along, or one even more beautiful. Look, what is that making everybody doff their hats along the whole line? Six white horses draw a fine coach. Who is that sitting within? The emperor and the empress. Are you surprised? Have you not seen this in Paris? Here one greets and shows not the least astonishment that they drive as private persons among private people—one is accustomed to it, and they know that they are as safe in the densest crush of the crowd as in their palace. Look, the hero of Aspern is also there. Do you see? It is that man in black, the one who goes with another in the equestrian avenue and is greeted by all. But just wait, we shall certainly see still others of high rank as they enter into and enjoy the pleasures of the day. There he goes behind the coach-and-six and joins with the day's procession of carriages, even as this hackney which pants by with its two laboring bays.

But let us now go down the avenue off to one side in order to see what else the Prater has to offer besides this flood of faces, dress and equipages so stupefying to the senses. Yet as we advance farther and farther, it seems as if it becomes even worse; the knot becomes tighter and quieter. To the left of the avenue are restaurants, the so-called Prater coffeehouses; from them come sounds of music; under the trees stand thousands of chairs overrun with a tangle of smartly dressed people—they talk, they laugh, they roar, they clink glasses, they call for the waiter—and up and down before your eyes winds the driving and rolling of gleaming carriages as far as the eye can see, as if the avenue had no end.

ADALBERT STIFTER
*Vienna and the Viennese in
Pictures from Life,* 1844

DAY IN
THE SUN

The Austrian free republic, established by the Treaty of Versailles in 1919, came to an end with the violently authoritative regime of Engelbert Dollfuss, who became chancellor in 1932. Dollfuss, irreconcilably opposed to the Anschluss with Germany and to National Socialism, was nevertheless assassinated in 1934, paving the way for Adolf Hitler. The extremes to which Vienna was reduced during the period are dramatically conveyed in this passage from a long poem on Vienna by Stephen Spender, the Oxford poet known for his poems of social protest who visited the city in the thirties.

The Executive

In order to create order, in order
To illustrate the truth that we are your ancestors
Let the generals wear their orders
Let the firemen dress like archdukes let the army
Be only one of six private armies
Let there be processions o let banners
Stream through the streets that anyhow look like
      pictures
Let no one disagree let Dollfuss
Fey, Stahremberg, the whole bloody lot
Appear frequently, shaking hands at street corners
Looking like bad sculptures of their photographs.
Let there be bands and stands and preparations
And grateful peasants in costumed deputations
Create the ghost of an emperor's coronation
Stalking the streets and holding up the trams.

The Unemployed

      Dispersed like idle points of a vague star:
Huddled on benches, nude at bathing places,
And made invisible by crucifying suns
Day after day, again with grief afire at night,
They do not watch what we show.
Their eyes are fixed upon an economic margin
Where the corn's starved by tares, where fluid grass
Trickles through rotted floors of senseless mills,
Where railway crossings with feeling, lifted wands
Are blistered, rails rust, bricks fall, and ivy
Smothers phallic chimneys.
                  Ask the unemployed
At pavement's edge, at brink of river
Why do you stare at us with the same indifference
As at a main road of wheels and legs and facts
Birth, death, the inexplicable irrelevance
Of lust? (Do not ask that woman
With dark eyes neglected, a demanding turn of the head
And hair of black silky beasts, because our life is
A cage of lightest aluminum bars
Beyond the strength of tigers, conquering what's most
      feared
With moral weakness.) But turn to boys

Your bought lovers, howitzer fodder, blazoned
Future; why do you play cards
In gutters, sulk, hands in pocket, strip naked
And bathe, hike, betray your girls?
Is history ungrateful? Do books
Ignore us? Can a government be unimportant?

We can read their bodies like advertisements
On hoardings, shouting with common answers.
Not saying, life is happy, unhappy is ill,
Death is reward, law just, but only
Life is life, body is body, a day
Is the sun: there is left only beauty
Of merest being, of swimming, of somehow not
        starving:
And merest beauty has a sun-tanned body
Available for uses, but only sold. Pathic
Strength of marble thighs, Greek chest, a torso
Without purposive veins travelling to hands.
"It is a daystream thick with many
"Laws, bombs, processions, handbills, church services,
"Straws doubtless golden float among the many
"But are indiscernible to a rich eye,
"A drowned eye." Politely, they stay away.

STEPHEN SPENDER
Vienna, 1935

A LOST WORLD OF CULTURE

Stefan Zweig, born and bred in the Vienna of Hugo von Hofmannstahl and Richard Strauss, earned early recognition as a playwright and essayist. After moving to Paris in 1904, where he made many friends in the literary world, then visiting London, Berlin, and the other great capitals of Western Europe, Zweig journeyed to India, Africa, and parts of America, gaining an extraordinarily wide world outlook before his return to Vienna just before World War I. The success of his biography of Marie Antoinette and his other works was matched by that of his autobiography, The World of Yesterday, *published in 1943, from which the following is excerpted.*

There is hardly a city in Europe where the drive towards cultural ideals was as passionate as it was in Vienna. Precisely because the monarchy, because Austria itself for centuries had been neither politically ambitious nor particularly successful in its military actions, the native pride had turned more strongly toward a desire for artistic supremacy. The most important and the most valuable provinces, German and Italian, Flemish and Walloon, had long since fallen away from the old Habsburg empire that had once ruled Europe; unsullied in its old glory, the capital had remained the treasure of the court, the preserver of a thousand-year-old tradition. The Romans had laid the first stones of this city, as a *castrum,* a fortress, an advance outpost to protect Latin civilization against the barbarians; and more than a thousand years later the attack of the Ottomans against the West shat-

tered against these walls. Here rode the Nibelungs, here the immortal Pleiades of music shone out over the world, Gluck, Haydn, Mozart, Beethoven, Schubert, Brahms, and Johann Strauss, here all the streams of European culture converged. At court, among the nobility, and among the people, the German was related in blood to the Slavic, the Hungarian, the Spanish, the Italian, the French, the Flemish; and it was the particular genius of this city of music that dissolved all the contrasts harmoniously into a new and unique thing, the Austrian, the Viennese. Hospitable and endowed with a particular talent for receptivity, the city drew the most diverse forces to it, loosened, propitiated, and pacified them. It was sweet to live here, in this atmosphere of spiritual conciliation, and subconsciously every citizen became supernational, cosmopolitan, a citizen of the world.

This talent for assimilation, for delicate and musical transitions, was already apparent in the external visage of the city. Growing slowly through the centuries, organically developing outward from inner circles, it was sufficiently populous, with its two millions, to yield all the luxury and all the diversity of a metropolis, and yet it was not so oversized as to be cut off from nature, like London or New York. The last houses of the city mirrored themselves in the mighty Danube or looked out over the wide plains, or dissolved themselves in gardens and fields, or climbed in gradual rises the last green wooded foothills of the Alps. One hardly sensed where nature began and where the city; one melted into the other without opposition, without contradiction. Within, however, one felt that the city had grown like a tree that adds ring upon ring, and instead of the old fortification walls the Ringstrasse encircled the treasured core with its splendid houses. Within, the old palaces of the court and the nobility spoke history in stone. Here Beethoven had played at the Lichnowskys', at the Esterhazys' Haydn had been a guest; there in the old University Haydn's *Creation* had resounded for the first time, the Hofburg had seen generations of emperors, and Schönbrunn had seen Napoleon. In the Stefansdom the united lords of Christianity had knelt in prayers of thanksgiving for the salvation of Europe from the Turks; countless great lights of science had been within the walls of the University. In the midst of all this, the new architecture reared itself proudly and grandly with glittering avenues and sparkling shops. But the old quarreled as little with the new as the chiseled stone with untouched nature.

Until our fourteenth or fifteenth year we still felt ourselves perfectly at home in school. We made fun of the teachers and we learned our lessons with cold curiosity. But then the hour struck when school began to bore and disturb us. A remarkable phenomenon had quietly taken place: we, who had entered the *Gymnasium* as ten-year-olds, had intellectually outgrown the school already, in the first four of our eight years. We felt instinctively that there was nothing more of importance to be learned from it, and that in many of the subjects which interested us we knew more than our poor teachers, who had not opened a book out of personal interest since their own student years. But there was another contrast which became more apparent from day to day: on the benches, where no more of us than our breeches was sitting, we heard nothing new or nothing that to us seemed worth knowing, and outside there was a city of a thousand attractions, a city with theaters, museums, bookstores, universities, music, a city in which each day brought new surprises. And so our pent-up desire for knowledge, our intellectual, artistic and sensuous inquisitiveness, which found no nourishment in school, passionately yearned for all that went on outside of school. At first only two or three of us discovered in themselves such artistic, literary and musical interests, then a dozen, and finally nearly all of us.

For among young people enthusiasm is a kind of catching phenomenon. In a class at school it infects one after another like a scarlet fever or measles, and while the neophytes, with childish, vain ambition, try to outdo each other as rapidly as possible in their knowledge, they lead each other on. It is therefore merely a matter of chance which direction these passions take: if there is a stamp collector in one class he will soon make a dozen as foolish as himself, and if three rave about dancers, the others will daily stand before the stagedoor of the Opera. Three years after us came a class which was possessed with a passion for football, and before ours there was another that was wholly devoted to Tolstoy or socialism. By chance I entered a class in which my comrades were art enthusiasts; and this may possibly have been decisive for the development of my life. In itself this enthusiasm for the theater, for literature and for art was quite natural in Vienna. The newspapers devoted special space to all the cultural events that took place in the city, and wherever we went, right and left, we heard the grown-ups discuss the opera or the Burgtheater. The pictures of the great actors were on display in all the stationery stores. Sport was still considered to be a brutal affair of which a student of the *Gymnasium* should rightly be ashamed, and the cinema with its mass ideals had not yet been invented. At home there was no opposition to be feared; literature and the theater belonged to the "innocent" passions, in contrast to playing cards or friendships with girls. Finally, my father, like all Viennese fathers, had also been smitten with the theater, and had attended the performance of *Lohengrin* under Richard Wagner with the same enthusiasm that we felt at the premières of Richard Strauss and Gerhart Hauptmann. For it was to be expected that we *Gymnasium* students should throng to each première; how ashamed we would have been before our more fortunate colleagues had we not been able to report every single detail on the morrow! Had our teachers not been completely indifferent, it would have occurred to them that on the afternoon of an important première—we had to stand in line at three o'clock to secure standing room, the only places available to us—two-thirds of all the students were taken with some mysterious illness. With strict attention they would also have discovered that the poems of Rilke were stuck between the covers of our Latin grammars, and that we used our mathematics notebooks to copy the loveliest poems out of books which we had borrowed. Daily we invented new techniques for using the dull school hours for our reading. While the teacher delivered his time-worn lecture about the "naïve and sentimental poetry" of Schiller, under our desks we read Nietzsche and Strindberg, whose names the good old man had never heard. A fever had come over us to know all, to be familiar with all

VER SACRVM

that occurred in every field of art and science. In the afternoon we pushed our way among the university students to listen to the lectures, we visited all of the art exhibitions, we went in to the anatomy classrooms to watch dissections. We sniffed at all and everything with inquisitive nostrils. We crept in to the rehearsals of the Philharmonic, we hunted about in the antique shops, we examined the booksellers' displays daily, so that we might know at once what had turned up since yesterday. And above all, we read! We read everything that came into our hands. We got books from all of the public libraries, and lent each other whatever we had been able to discover. But the coffeehouse was still the best place to keep up with everything new.

In order to understand this, it must be said that the Viennese coffee-house is a particular institution which is not comparable to any other in the world. As a matter of fact, it is a sort of democratic club to which admission costs the small price of a cup of coffee. Upon payment of this mite every guest can sit for hours on end, discuss, write, play cards, receive his mail, and, above all, can go through an unlimited number of newspapers and magazines. In the better-class Viennese coffeehouse all the Viennese newspapers were available, and not the Viennese alone, but also those of the entire German Reich, the French and the English, the Italian and the American papers, and in addition all of the important literary and art magazines of the world, the *Revue de France* no less than the *Neue Rundschau*, the *Studio*, and the *Burlington Magazine.* And so we knew everything that took place in the world at first hand, we learned about every book that was published, and every production no matter where it occurred; and we compared the notices in every newspaper. Perhaps nothing has contributed as much to the intellectual mobility and the international orientation of the Austrian as that he could keep abreast of all world events in the coffeehouse, and at the same time discuss them in the circle of his friends. For, thanks to the collectivity of our interests, we followed the *orbis pictus* of artistic events not with two, but with twenty and forty eyes. . . .

 · Buchs [on the Swiss frontier] had afforded me an exciting moment a year earlier; now, upon my return [in 1918], a no less memorable one awaited me at Feldkirch, the Austrian border station. Upon alighting I became aware of an odd restlessness among the customs officers and police. They paid small attention to us and made their inspection in a most negligent manner; plainly something important was to happen. At last came the bell that announced the approach of a train from the Austrian side. The police lined up, the officials piled out of their offices, their womenfolk, evidently in the know, crowded together on the platform. I was particularly struck by an old lady in black with her two daughters, from her carriage and clothes presumably an aristocrat. She was visibly excited and constantly pressed her handkerchief to her eyes.

Slowly, almost majestically, it seemed, the train rolled near, a special sort of train, not the customary, shabby, weather-beaten kind, but with spacious black cars, a train de luxe. The locomotive stopped. There was a perceptible stir among the lines of those waiting but I was still in the dark. Then I recognized behind the plate glass window of the car Emperor Karl, the last emperor of Austria standing with his black-clad wife, Empress Zita. I was startled; the last emperor of Austria, heir of the Habsburg dynasty which had ruled for seven hundred years, was forsaking his realm! He had refused to abdicate formally, yet the Republic granted every honor on the departure which it compelled rather than submitted. The tall serious man at the window was having a last look at the hills and homes, at the people of his land. The historic moment was doubly shocking to me who had grown up in the tradition of the Empire, whose first song at school had been the *Kaiserlied* and who had taken the military oath to obey "on land, at sea, and in the air" this serious and thoughtful looking man in mufti. Innumerable times had I seen the old emperor in the long since legendary splendor of elaborate celebrations; I had seen him on the great staircase of Schönbrunn, surrounded by his family and brilliantly uniformed generals, receiving the homage of the eighty thousand Viennese school children, massed on the broad green plain, singing, their thin voices united in touching chorus, Haydn's *Gott erhalte.* I had seen him at the Court ball, at the Théâtre Paré performances in glittering array, and again in Ischl, riding to the hunt in a green Tyrolean hat; I had seen him marching devoutly, with bowed head, in the Corpus Christi procession to the Cathedral of St. Stephen, and then the catafalque, on that foggy, wet winter day in the midst of war, which bore the aged man to his last rest in the Capuchin crypt. "The Kaiser!" From earliest childhood we had learned to pronounce those words reverently for they embodied all of power and wealth and symbolized Austria's imperishability. And now I saw his heir, the last emperor, banished from his country. From century to century the glorious line of Habsburg had passed the Imperial globe and crown from hand to hand, and this was the minute of its end. All of those who stood about sensed history, world history, in this tragic sight. The gendarmes, the police, the soldiery were embarrassed and looked abashed because uncertain whether the traditional recognition was still in order, the women hardly dared to look up, all were silent and thus the faint sobbing of the old lady in mourning who had come heaven knows what distance, only to see "her" emperor once more, was plainly audible. At last the conductor gave the signal. Everybody stared up mechanically, the irrevocable instant had come. The locomotive started with a violent jerk as if it too had to overcome a disinclination, and slowly the train withdrew. The officials followed it with a respectful gaze, after which, with that air of embarrassment which is observable at funerals, they returned to their respective stations. It was the moment in which the almost millenary monarchy really ended. I knew it was a different Austria, a different world, to which I was returning.

STEFAN ZWEIG
The World of Yesterday, 1943

160

REFERENCE

Chronology of Viennese History

167	Marcus Aurelius wins victory over the Marcomanni
180	Marcus Aurelius dies in Vindobona, site of modern Vienna
962	Otto II crowned by Pope Gregory as Holy Roman Emperor
976	Luitpold of Babenberg founds Klosterneuburg, site of the Hofburg
1135	Babenbergs gain possession of Vienna
1137	Vienna receives the status of a *civitas*
1156	Vienna becomes a duchy
1241	Vienna threatened by the Mongols
1246	Frederick II, last of the Babenbergs, dies
1272	Rudolf von Habsburg chosen Holy Roman Emperor
1278	Ottocar Premysl of Bohemia defeated by Rudolf von Habsburg in battle of the Marchfeld
1282	Vienna becomes capital of the Habsburgs
1340	Consecration of Gothic choir of St. Stephen's
1359	South tower of St. Stephen's begun
1365	University of Vienna founded by Rudolf IV
1439	South tower of St. Stephen's completed
1440	Frederick III elected Holy Roman Emperor
1477	Maximilian (later emperor) marries Mary of Burgundy
1482	Vienna captured by Matthias Corvinus, king of Hungary
1485	Maximilian drives the Hungarians out of Vienna
1493	Death of Frederick III; Maximilian I becomes emperor and marries Bianca Sforza
1496	Hofkapelle, the Imperial Orchestra, founded by Maximilian I; Maximilian I's son Philip marries Joanna of Castile and Aragon
1516	Maximilian I's grandson Charles succeeds to the Spanish throne
1519	Death of Maximilian I
1521	Charles V elected Holy Roman Emperor; bans Martin Luther
1526	Charles V marries Isabella of Portugal
1529	Siege of Vienna by the Turks under Suleiman II
1545	Council of Trent
1547	Titian paints Charles V after battle of Mühlberg
1555	Diet of Augsburg gives German princes right to choose their religion
1558	Ferdinand I becomes emperor on abdication of Charles V
1576	Rudolf II elected emperor
1598	Construction of the Danube Canal
1619	Ferdinand II elected emperor
1652	The "Reformation Patent" confirms the Counterreformation
1658	Leopold I elected emperor
1671	Turks defeated in battle of Lepanto
1679	The Great Plague; Augustinian friar Abraham a Sancta Clara calls on the Viennese to repent
1683	Turkish siege of Vienna under Grand Vizier Kara Mustafa defeated
1684	Kolschitzky establishes first coffee house in Vienna
1697	Prince Eugene of Savoy becomes field marshal following victory over the Turks at Zenta
1705	Leopold I dies; accession of Joseph I; Academy of Fine Arts inaugurated
1706	Park of Schoenbrunn laid out; Kärntnertor Theatre, for impromptu plays and ballets, started
1711	Charles VI becomes emperor
1713	Treaty of Utrecht; the "Pragmatic Sanction" established, ensuring Habsburg succession and Maria Theresia as rightful heiress
1718	Porcelain factory established at Rossau
1720	Palais Kinsky built by Lucas von Hildebrandt for Count Philip Daun
1723	Belvedere Palace, built by Lucas von Hildebrandt, completed
1734	Church of St. Charles Borromeo completed
1740	Accession of Maria Theresia as Holy Roman Empress; Frederick II, king of Prussia, starts the War of the Austrian Succession
1741	Battle of Mollwitz secures Silesia for Prussia
1745	Francis of Lorraine recognized as Holy Roman Emperor, co-Regent with his wife, Maria Theresia
1751	Maria Theresia introduces theater censorship
1754	Christoph Gluck appointed *Kapellmeister*
1757	Defeat of Frederick II at battle of Kolin by Maria Theresia's commander Leopold Daun
1762	Gluck's *Orpheus and Euridice* performed in the Old Burgtheater
1765	Death of Francis, who is succeeded by Joseph II as co-Regent with Maria Theresia and Holy Roman Emperor
1770	Maria Theresia's daughter Maria Antonia, called Marie Antoinette, marries the French Dauphin
1777	Joseph II opens the Prater, until then an imperial preserve, to the public
1780	Death of Maria Theresia
1781	Joseph II lifts theater censorship
1782	First performance of Wolfgang Amadeus Mozart's *Abduction from the Seraglio*
1783	Emmanuel Schikaneder becomes director of the Kärntnertor Theatre
1787	Death of Gluck

1790	Joseph II dies; succeeded by Leopold II
1791	Mozart's *Die Zauberflöte* (*The Magic Flute*) performed; Mozart dies
1792	Leopold II dies; succeeded by his son Francis, the last Holy Roman Emperor; Ludwig van Beethoven comes to Vienna
1797	Franz Joseph Haydn's *Creation* oratorio performed
1804	Beethoven's *Eroica* Symphony first performed
1805	Battle of Austerlitz; Napoleon occupies Vienna; first performance of Beethoven's *Fidelio*
1806	Dissolution of the Holy Roman Empire; Francis I becomes emperor of Austria
1809	Charles, Archduke of Austria, defeats Napoleon at battle of Aspern but is defeated in battle of Wagram; Napoleon reenters Vienna; Prince Metternich becomes foreign minister; death of Haydn
1810	Napoleon weds Marie Louise, daughter of Francis I
1811	Napoleon's son, the Prince of Parma, is born
1813	Battle of Leipzig; Napoleon is defeated by the allied Austrians, Prussians, and Russians
1814	Napoleon abdicates and is exiled to Elba
1815	Congress of Vienna; battle of Waterloo; Napoleon imprisoned at St. Helena
1824	First performance of Beethoven's Ninth Symphony
1827	Beethoven dies
1828	Franz Schubert dies
1835	Francis I dies; succeeded by Ferdinand I
1837	First Austrian railway, the *Kaiser-Ferdinands Nordbahn*, opened
1842	Vienna Philharmonic Orchestra founded
1848	Revolution of 1848; Prince Metternich forced to resign; Ferdinand I issues manifesto approving a new Constitution, then abdicates in favor of his nephew, Franz Joseph
1849	Johann Strauss the Elder dies
1850	Vienna becomes a self-governing municipality
1857	Franz Joseph issues decree to demolish Vienna's fortifications; competition announced for the design of the new Ringstrasse
1859	Battle of Solferino; Austrian empire loses Italy
1861	Jews given voting rights
1862	Viennese debut of Johannes Brahms
1863	The Heinrichhof, first of the palatial apartment houses on the Ringstrasse, opened
1864	*Neue Freie Presse* founded
1865	The Ringstrasse opened for use
1866	Battle of Königgratz (Sadowa); Austrians driven out of Germany; première of *Blue Danube* by Johann Strauss the Younger

1867	*Neue Wiener Tageblatt* founded; Maximilian, emperor of Mexico, executed by firing squad; emancipation of Austrian Jews
1868	Freedom of worship guaranteed to non-Catholics
1869	Opera House opened with Mozart's *Don Giovanni*
1873	World Exposition
1874	First performance of *Die Fledermaus* by Johann Strauss the Younger
1884	The Universität, last of the great Ringstrasse buildings, inaugurated
1889	Suicide of Archduke Rudolph
1893	Otto Wagner wins competition for the new development of Vienna; Anton Bruckner dies
1897	Franz Joseph ratifies Karl Lueger as mayor of Vienna; Theodor Herzl founds the Zionist weekly *Die Welt*
1898	First *Secession* exhibition, organized by Gustav Klimt, leader of the modernist movement; assassination of Empress Elizabeth in Geneva
1900	Sigmund Freud's *The Interpretation of Dreams* published
1902	Opening of the Vienna Underground Railway
1904	Otto Wagner builds the first functional building, of concrete, steel, and glass
1905	First performance of Franz Lehar's *The Merry Widow*
1908	Klimt's *The Kiss* exhibited at the Kunstschau
1911	*Die Rosenkavalier* by Richard Strauss performed
1914	Archduke Franz Ferdinand assassinated; World War I begins
1916	Death of Franz Joseph, who is succeeded by Karl I of Austria
1918	Abdication of Karl I as emperor of Austria and king of Hungary
1921	Vienna becomes a Land in the Federal Republic
1922	League of Nations guarantees the independence of Austria
1932	Engelbert Dollfuss appointed chancellor of the Austrian Republic by the predominant Christian Socialist party
1933	Dollfuss given dictatorial powers
1934	Dollfuss assassinated by an Austrian Nazi
1938	Dollfuss's successor, Kurt von Schuschnigg, finally yields to Adolf Hitler's *Anschluss*; Austria becomes part of the Third Reich
1939	World War II begins
1945	Soviet troops occupy bomb-damaged Vienna; Second Austrian Republic proclaimed; Theodor Körner elected Burgomeister of Vienna
1955	Austrian State Treaty signed in the Upper Belvedere, ending Allied occupation of Vienna
1979	Vienna United Nations International Center opened.

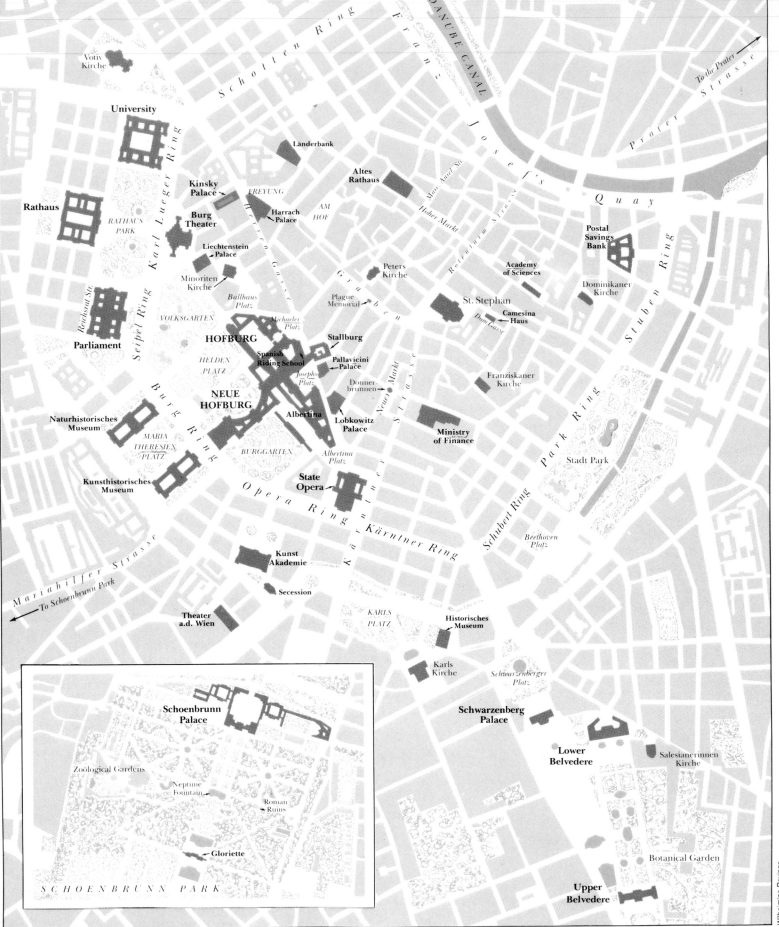

Votiv Kirche

University

Rathaus

RATHAUS PARK

Karl Lueger Ring

Kinsky Palace

Burg Theater

FREYUNG

Harrach Palace

Liechtenstein Palace

Minoriten Kirche

Seipel Ring

Reichsrat Str.

Parliament

Ballhaus Platz

VOLKSGARTEN

Michaeler Platz

HOFBURG

Spanish Riding School

HELDEN PLATZ

Josephs Platz

NEUE HOFBURG

Burg Ring

Naturhistorisches Museum

MARIA THERESIEN PLATZ

Kunsthistorisches Museum

BURGGARTEN

Albertina

Stallburg

Pallavicini Palace

Donner brunnen

Lobkowitz Palace

Albertina Platz

State Opera

Opera Ring

Kärntner Ring

Kunst Akademie

Secession

Mariahilfer Strasse

To Schoenbrunn Park

Theater a.d. Wien

KARLS PLATZ

Karls Kirche

Schollen Ring

Frans Josef's

DANUBE CANAL

To the Prater

Prater Strasse

Quay

Länderbank

Altes Rathaus

AM HOF

Hoher Markt

Marc Aurel Str.

Rotenturm Strasse

Peters Kirche

Plague Memorial

Graben

St. Stephan

Dom Gasse

Neuer Markt

Kärntner Strasse

Academy of Sciences

Camesina Haus

Franziskaner Kirche

Ministry of Finance

Postal Savings Bank

Stuben Ring

Dominikaner Kirche

Park Ring

Stadt Park

Schubert Ring

Beethoven Platz

Historisches Museum

Schwarzenberg Platz

Schwarzenberg Palace

Lower Belvedere

Salesianerinnen Kirche

Botanical Garden

Upper Belvedere

Schoenbrunn Palace

Zoölogical Gardens

Neptune Fountain

Roman Ruins

Gloriette

SCHOENBRUNN PARK

Wilhelmina Reyinga

For almost six hundred years as the capital of the Habsburg empire, Vienna was a highly fortified city, tightly circumscribed by a ring of bastions. It was not until 1857, nearly fifty years after these fortifications had been proved entirely useless by Napoleon's easy entry into Vienna, that the emperor Franz Joseph ordered the ramparts razed and work begun on the famous Ringstrasse—a development of monumental public buildings, avenues, and parks that is one of the outstanding achievements of nineteenth-century European city planning. Happily, it was due to this long delay in modern reconstruction that the so-called Inner City was preserved; it is here that most of the monuments of Vienna's past survive, particularly from the zenith of its cultural brilliance in the Baroque era.

The Inner City, called the *Alt Stadt*, with its maze of narrow streets dating back to medieval times and earlier, is intersected on a north-south axis by **Kärntner Strasse,** a main thoroughfare with fashionable shops and elegant restaurants, brilliantly illuminated at night. Known since the thirteenth century as a shopping district, Kärntner Strasse at its northern end terminates at **St. Stephen's Cathedral,** which is Vienna's most imposing landmark, visible from every part of the city. St. Stephen's was first a Romanesque church, dedicated in 1147; then after a fire in 1258, it was rebuilt in Gothic style (1290–1440), although retaining its original Romanesque façade—the Giant's Doorway (*Riesentor*) and the towers at the west end. At the east end stands its majestic south tower, a free-standing pure Gothic steeple 448 feet high (completed in 1439). The north tower, never completed, rises to barely the height of the west towers; it houses the famous twenty-ton "Pummarin" bell, originally cast from Turkish cannons in 1711, and recast after its destruction in World War II. St. Stephen's distinctive polychrome tile roof, which was also completely destroyed in the 1945 gutting of the cathedral, has been immaculately restored. The late Gothic interior, with its soaring columns and articulated vaulting (completed in 1440), is embellished by a number of notable monuments—including the carved and painted wood Wiener-Neustadt Altarpiece in the Lady Chapel, the majestic red marble tomb of the fifteenth-century emperor Frederick III, and the intricately carved stone pulpit (*c.* 1510) by Anton Pilgram in a flamboyant Gothic style that anticipates the fantasies of Viennese Baroque.

Habsburg power and Baroque splendor are vividly manifest in the extensive architectural ensemble of the **Hofburg,** or Imperial Palace. Residence and administrative center of the emperors, the Hofburg was built progressively over the centuries. Begun around 1220 as a fortress-like castle, its original courtyard survives today in the **Schweizerhof** (or Swiss Court, as it is now known), entered through the imposing Renaissance-style Schweizertor (Swiss Guard's Gate, erected in 1552). The court gives access to the Hofburg's Gothic chapel (**Hofkapelle,** *c.* 1459), where since the early eighteenth century the sacred music of Haydn, Mozart, Beethoven, and Bruckner has been heard.

The larger court outside the Schweizerhof is enclosed on the northwest by the Chancellery wing, with a resplendent Baroque façade (begun in 1723) by the architect Lucas von Hildebrandt. Designed by an equally famous exponent of Viennese Baroque, Johann Bernhard Fischer von Erlach, the **National Library** (formerly Court Library), facing Josefplatz, has a domed interior which is one of the most magnificent Baroque halls anywhere. On the north side of Josefplatz—named after the emperor Joseph II, who is commemorated there by Anton Zauner's imposing equestrian statue (1806)—is the **Redoutensaal** (Ball Room), and beyond that, to the right, the entrance to the **Stallburg,** an arcaded court regarded as one of the finest Renaissance buildings in Austria. Once the imperial stables, with apartments on the upper floors, it was converted by the archduke Leopold William in the seventeenth century to house his famous collection of Old Master paintings and art objects which today constitutes the nucleus of the collections in the Kunsthistorisches Museum. Adjacent to the Stallburg, across the Reitschul Gasse, is the **Spanish Riding School,** another architectural masterpiece by Fischer von Erlach, used to this day for *Haute École* equestrian exercises on the celebrated white Lippizaner stallions.

The stately, curving façade of the **Hofburg** on Michaelerplatz was built by Ferdinand Kirschner, after designs by Fischer von Erlach. Its central entrance leads to the former imperial apartments and the magnificent collection of porcelain and silver used for the court service. Across an inner court is the Habsburg Treasury, containing goldwork, gems, and other relics dating from the Middle Ages onward; and at the southern end of the Hofburg is the **Albertina,** the famous collection of graphic art assembled by Duke Albert of Saxony-Teschen, amounting to almost a million Old Master drawings.

Facing the National Library on the street side of Josefplatz is the **Fries-Pallavicini Palace** with its Neoclassical caryatid porch (1783–84), which, together with the stately **Lobkowitz Palace** (1685–87) one block to the south, became a center of Viennese musical life in the early nineteenth century. Prince Joseph von Lobkowitz was Beethoven's greatest patron, and it was in his house that the *Pastoral Symphony* and other Beethoven compositions were first played.

Among other princely residences that give such a distinctive air of Baroque splendor to the Inner City are the palace on Ballhausplatz off the north end of the Hofburg, which served as Prince

Metternich's residence during his years in Vienna; the **Liechtenstein Palace** (*c.* 1700) on nearby Bank Gasse; the **Daun-Kinsky Palace** further north, built by Lucas von Hildebrandt; and Prince Eugene of Savoy's town house in Himmelpfortgasse (now the **Ministry of Finance**), with the overpowering Michelangelesque caryatids on its monumental interior staircase (1695–98).

Outside the city fortifications, in what was then open country to the south, Prince Eugene built the **Belvedere,** a sort of double palace on terraced formal gardens. This elaborate estate includes the "Lower Belvedere" (1714–16), originally intended as a summer residence, and the "Upper Belvedere" (1721–22), a showplace for imperial ceremonies. Both buildings were designed by Hildebrandt, and the Upper Belvedere is regarded as his masterpiece. It is an outstanding example of Baroque architecture, its fantastic roofline suggesting Turkish tents, in honor of Prince Eugene's victory over the Turks. The Upper Belvedere is on higher ground and commands a breathtaking view of the city. It has been the site of many historic functions, including the signing of the 1955 state treaty restoring Austria's sovereignty and making it a permanently neutral state.

The Baroque charm of the Belvedere is shared by the nearby Church of St. Charles Borromeo, the **Karlskirche,** with its oval dome, exotically roofed side pavilions, and twin west towers that look like minarets. Built by Fischer von Erlach for the emperor Charles VI in fulfillment of a vow for the ending of the plague in 1713, it expresses the triumph of the Counter Reformation in genial Baroque terms. The towers are clearly derived from Trajan's column in Rome, but here their spiral reliefs depict events in the life of the great reformer saint.

Further outside the Inner City, on even more extensive grounds than the Belvedere, stands **Schoenbrunn Palace,** the former imperial summer residence. It was built in 1694 by the emperor Leopold I from plans by Fischer von Erlach on a scale to rival Versailles. During the reign of Maria Theresia the palace was reconstructed by the Italian architect Nicolas Pacassi, with additions which include the Porcelain Room (1760) and the Millionen Room, both remarkable examples of Rococo ornamentation, reflecting the queen's marked taste for Chinoiserie. The immense park of Schoenbrunn, covering an area almost the size of the Inner City itself, was laid out by the Viennese architect Ferdinand von Hohenberg in a grid of rectangularly and diagonally intersecting *allées* bordered by twenty-foot-high clipped hedges that screen whole areas of freely growing trees and afford unexpected perspectives of the palace and other structures scattered throughout the park—the Gloriette at the far end, the Neptune Fountain, the "Roman Ruins." It remains one of the best preserved eighteenth-century parks in Europe.

Another of Vienna's famous parks is the **Prater,** an immense area of woods and open meadows to the east of the city, between two branches of the Danube. It was originally an imperial game preserve, started in the sixteenth century by the emperor Maximilian II. Its celebrated **Hauptallee** (main avenue) was laid out in 1537–38, leading to the Lusthaus at the far end. The benevolent emperor Joseph II opened the park to the public in 1777 and it immediately became one of Vienna's most popular out-of-town haunts with cafés, music, and every kind of outdoor recreation (see pp. 151–154).

Within the Inner City, the pervasive Baroque idiom everywhere disseminates its sense of splendor, charm, and brilliance. Paralleling the monumental grandeur of the palaces are not only the ecclesiastic pomp of churches like **Peterskirche** (by Hildebrandt, 1708) off the **Graben** and the stately monumentality of the **Academy of Science** (1753) on Universitätsplatz, but also the theatrical interior of the **Jesuit Church** (1628–1705, now Universität Church), the flamboyantly florid **Pestsäule** (1694) on the Graben, the fluid virtuosity of **Donner's Neuer Markt** and **Andromeda Fountains,** the cadenced rhythms of the **Dominican Church** organ, evoking Mozart or Haydn melodies.

These characteristics of a courtly, aristocratic society penetrate the town houses of the middle classes, lending a note of gaiety and light everywhere along the narrow streets of the Inner City. A typical example in the "Old Quarter" near the cathedral is the **Camesina Haus** on the Domgasse. It belonged to a Swiss-Italian named Alberto Camesina, a prominent stucco worker; not only is its façade typically decorated with stucco moldings and cornices, but also a room on its *piano nobile* has a stucco ceiling decorated with nymphs and amorettos. Mozart lived in the Camesina Haus from 1784 to 1787, and in this room he wrote *The Marriage of Figaro,* played quartets with Haydn and his friends, and met Beethoven in the spring of 1787. Even more modest houses have a certain elegance by virtue of architectural forms which were standard in the art of stucco decoration, such as vaulted ceilings, cornices, moldings, and walls made to look like stone masonry.

After the Revolution of 1848, in an age of growing liberalism, the need for open space for the rapidly expanding urban society dictated the demolition of Vienna's encircling fortifications and the development of the extensive **Ringstrasse** complex of parks and public buildings. The buildings were now to be centers of constitutional government and higher culture, rather than palaces and churches. Likewise, abandoning the

Baroque, the diversity of architectural styles of the great public structures erected between 1858 and 1888 are in large measure based on the principle of borrowing a historical style appropriate to the function of a given building. To evoke the parliamentary integration of peers and people, the **Parliament** building (1874–83) facing the Hofburg across the **Volksgarten** was designed as a Greek temple by the Danish architect Theophil Hansen. Next to it to the north, the **Rathaus** was built in pure Gothic like a Flemish town hall (by Friedrich Schmidt, 1872–83), to symbolize the freedom of Vienna as a medieval commune; and the adjacent **University** (1873–84), in the Renaissance style, to recall the beginnings of modern humanist learning at the universities of Padua, Genoa, and Bologna. The architect of the University was Heinrich Ferstel, who some fifteen years before had won the competition for the nearby **Votivkirche**—not a part of the Ringstrasse, but built to commemorate the escape of the emperor Franz Joseph from an unsuccessful assassination attempt in 1853. The Votivkirche also typifies the convention of expressing the function of a building by an applicable historical style. The church faithfully follows the form of a French High Gothic cathedral, although not in type of construction, as the upper parts of its two symmetrical spires are in openwork iron instead of stone.

Returning to the Ringstrasse development, the **Museums of Art History (Kunsthistorisches Museum)** and **Natural History,** facing each other on the Maria Theresien Platz, revert to a powerful neo-Baroque style of architecture. They are the work of the German architect Gottfried Semper, who had conceived the idea of a great "Imperial Forum" that would extend across the Ringstrasse to the Hofburg, to which would be added two new wings connected with the museums by bridges over the Ringstrasse. As it happened, only the southern wing of the Hofburg was built, the **Neue Hofburg** (also by Semper, with the collaboration of the Viennese architect Carl Hasenauer), with a stately inwardly curving Baroque façade. The Neue Hofburg today houses important collections of ancient art, arms and armor, and musical instruments. The northern wing never having been built, the fortuitous result is that, instead of an "Imperial Forum," the Heldenpark at its northern end merges with the Volksgarten, affording an unbroken park area all the way to the **Burgtheater** (also in a Baroque style, by Semper and Hasenauer).

On the southern side of the Neue Hofburg is another open space, the **Burggarten,** and then a block away, the **State Opera** (or Hofoper), at the intersection of the Ringstrasse with Kärntnerstrasse. The Opera was the first of the new public buildings erected on the Ringstrasse (by August von Siccardsburg and Eduard von der Null, 1861–69). In what may be called a sort of "free Renaissance" style, both in its exterior mass and in its interior "Imperial Stairway," it is perhaps the most impressive of the Ringstrasse structures.

The new buildings in the vast circular space of the Ringstrasse were by no means all public edifices. By far the majority were large apartment houses for the well-to-do and the upwardly moving middle class. The proceeds of the land sales provided the capital for the public buildings, according to the recent historian of Vienna, Carl E. Schorske. As multiple-unit dwellings, these apartment houses were given palatial façades and interior staircases of imposing grandeur, to look like palaces in the Inner City, where traditionally the upper floors were rented for apartments. Many were designed by the same architects as the public buildings, and their collective effect lends an aristo-cratic character to whole quarters, such as the **Schwarzenbergerplatz** (built by Ferstel, and mostly owned by the archduke Ludwig Victor and the banker von Wertheim) and the **Reichsratstrasse,** extending behind the Parliament, with its neo-Renaissance façades recalling the exclusive Herren Gasse in the Inner City.

One architect who in his earlier years had participated in the Ringstrasse development was Otto Wagner. Even in his early work, in which he conformed with the prevailing neo-Baroque, there are premonitions of the functional modernism for which he became known (**Austrian Länderbank,** 1882–84). But after winning an 1893 competition for the wider development plan of Vienna and its extensive suburbs and starting work on the **Vienna Underground Railway** (1894–1901), the primacy of utility and engineered structure over the "style architecture" of the Ringstrasse buildings began to emerge. This can be seen not only in the new materials employed in his subway stations (for instance, the **Unter-Döbling Station,** 1895–96), but also in the "functional honesty" and Jugendstil ornament of the **Wienzeile** apartment houses (1888–89) at the intersection with Köstlergasse, and the lean elegance of his **Postal Savings Bank** (1904–06) on Dominikaner Bastei.

Wagner was not alone in his modernism. He belonged to the group of avant-garde Viennese artists called the Secession, led by the painter Gustav Klimt. They called themselves Secessionists because they had "seceded" from the Künstlerhaus, Vienna's Art Academy. Symbolic of the movement is the little **Secession** building, the pioneering gallery of modern art in the Gedreidemarkt, designed by Josef Olbrich, one of Wagner's most gifted followers. Over its entrance in bold raised lettering is the motto: "To the age, its art; to art, its freedom."

Selected Bibliography

Barea, Ilsa. *Vienna.* New York: Alfred A. Knopf, 1966.

Brion, Marcel. *Daily Life in the Vienna of Mozart and Schubert.* Translated by Jean Stewart. New York: The Macmillan Co., 1962.

Comini, Alessandra. *The Fantastic Art of Vienna.* New York: Alfred A. Knopf, 1978.

Crankshaw, Edward. *The Habsburgs: Portrait of a Dynasty.* New York: Viking Press, 1971.

Crankshaw, Edward. *Maria Theresa.* New York: Viking Press, 1969.

Freud, Martin. Glory reflected: Sigmund Freud, man and father. New York: Vanguard, 1958.

Jacob, Heinrich Eduard. Johann Strauss, Father and Son, a century of light music. Translated by Marguerite Wolff. New York: Crown, 1939.

Macartney, C. A. *The Habsburg Empire*, 1790–1918. London: Weidenfeld and Nicolson, 1968.

McGuigan, Dorothy Gies. *The Habsburgs.* Garden City: Doubleday, 1966.

Morton, Frederic. *A nervous splendor: Vienna 1888–1889.* Boston: Little Brown and Company, 1979.

Mozart, Wolfgang Amadeus. *The Letters of Mozart and his Family.* Translated and edited by Emily Anderson. London: Macmillan & Co., 1938.

Nebehay, Christian M. *Ver Sacrum 1898–1903.* New York: Rizzoli International Publications, Inc., 1977.

Novotny, Fritz. *Gustav Klimt, with a catalogue raisonné of his painting.* New York: Praeger, 1968.

Pick, Robert. *The Last Days of Imperial Vienna.* New York: Dial Press, 1976.

Prawy, Marcel. *The Vienna Opera.* New York: Praeger, 1970.

Rath, R. John. *The Viennese Revolution of 1848.* Austin, Texas: University of Texas Press, 1957.

Schmidt-Görg, Joseph, and Schmidt, Hans, editors. *Ludwig van Beethoven.* New York, London: *Praeger Publishers, Inc.,* 1970.

Schorske, Carl E. *Fin-de-Siècle Vienna: politics and culture.* New York: Alfred A. Knopf, 1980.

Stoye, John. *The Siege of Vienna.* New York: Holt, Rinehart and Winston, 1965.

Taylor, A. J. P. *The Habsburg Monarchy,* 1809–1918. London: Macmillan & Co., 1941.

Redlich, Josef. *Emperor Francis Josef of Austria: a Biography.* New York: The Macmillan Company, 1929.

Webster, Charles Kingsley. *The Congress of Vienna, 1814–1815.* London: Oxford University Press, 1918.

Wechsberg, Joseph. *The Waltz Emperors, the life and times and music of the Strauss family.* New York: G. P. Putnam's Sons, 1973.

Zweig, Stefan. *The World of Yesterday; an autobiography.* New York: The Viking Press, 1943.

Acknowledgments and Picture Credits

The Editors make grateful acknowledgment for the use of excerpted material from the following works:

Correspondence entre l'Empereur Maximilien et Marguerite d'Autriche, 1509–1519. Paris, Jules Renouard, 1839, reprint 1966. The excerpted letter appearing on page 138 was translated by Dr. Albert Wolohojian.

Das Jahr 1683 und der folgende grosse Türkenkriege, by Onno Klopp. Graz, Verlags Buchhandlung Sturia, 1882. The excerpted letter appearing on page 139 was translated by Beatrice La Farge.

The Complete Letters of Lady Mary Wortley Montagu, edited by Robert Halsband. Oxford University Press, 1902. The excerpts appearing on pages 139–141 are reproduced by permission of Oxford University Press.

Continental Travels, 1770–1772, by Dr. Charles Burney. Compiled from his *Journals* . . . by Cedric Howard Glover. London and Glasgow, Blackie & Son Ltd., 1927. The excerpted passage appearing on pages 141–143 is reproduced by permission of Blackie & Son Ltd.

Letters of Mozart and His Family. Translated by Emily Anderson. London, Macmillan & Company, 1938. The excerpted letter appearing on pages 143–144 is reproduced by permission of Macmillan & Company.

Anecdotal Recollections of the Vienna Congress, by Comte Auguste de La Garde-Cambonas. Paris, 1820. Translation, London, Chapman & Hall Ltd., 1902. The excerpt appearing on pages 144–146 is from the Chapman & Hall edition.

Travels from Vienna through Lower Hungary, by Richard Bright. Edinburgh, Constable & Co., 1818. The excerpt appears on pp. 146–148.

Vienna and the Austrians, by Frances Trollope. London, Richard Bentley, 1837. The excerpt appears on 148–150.

Austria: Vienna, Prague, Hungary, Bohemia and the Danube, by J. G. Kohl. Translation from the German. London, Chapman & Hall, 1844. The excerpt appears on pages 150–151.

Der Prater, by Adalbert Stifter, from *Wien und die Wiener in Bildern aus dem Leben.* Pesth, Bei Gustav Heckenast, 1844. The excerpt appearing on pages 151–154 was translated by Beatrice La Farge.

Vienna, by Stephen Spender. New York, Random House, 1935. The excerpt appearing on pages 155–156 is reproduced by permission of Random House.

The World of Yesterday, by Stefan Zweig. New York, Viking Press, 1943. The excerpt appearing on pages 156–160 is reproduced by permission of Viking Press.

The Editors are particularly grateful to:

Foster V. Grunfeld for his preliminary research on the main text, to Barbara Pflaum-Gebhardt for her photographs of modern Vienna, to Beatrice La Farge for her translations from German texts, and to Dr. Albert Wolohojian for his translation from Old French. In addition the Editors would like to thank Charlie Holland, New York, Friederike Zeitlhofer, Austrian Institute of Cultural Affairs, New York, and Renate Kams, Newsweek Bureau, Bonn.

Many of the modern photographs of Vienna are the work of Barbara Pflaum-Gebhardt. The title or description of all other illustrations appears after the page number (boldface), *followed by its location or the name of the photographer* (in parentheses). *The following abbreviations are used:*

(BP)——(Barbara Pflaum-Gebhardt)
BONV——Bildarchiv Österreichische Nationalbibliothek, Vienna
HMSW——Historisches Museen der Stadt Wien
KMV——Kunsthistorisches Museum, Vienna

HALF-TITLE Symbol by Jay J. Smith TITLEPAGE (BP) **9–15** (BP) **16–17** Maximilian Lenz, *The Ringstrasse at Night*, 1898. Albertina, Vienna

CHAPTER 1 **18** and subsequent chapter openers: *Ver Sacrum*, Vienna, 1898–1903. **20** Venus of Willendorf, c. 20,000 B.C. Naturhistorisches Museum, Vienna **21** (BP) **22** Carnuntum. (Meyer) **24** top & **25** Abbey of Melk. (Marvin E. Newman) **24** bottom (BP) **26** Tomb of Frederick III, St. Stephen's. (Meyer) **27** Anton Pilgram, St. Stephen's. (Hubmann) **28** Stained-glass window of Emperor Rudolf I, 14th century. HMSW **29** B. Strigel, *Maximilian I and Family*. Academia de San Fernando, Madrid (Oroñoz) **30–31** Hans Burgkmair and A. Dürer, *Triumph of Maximilian I*, 1526. 1884 edition. **32** Austrian National Library, 1722. (Erich Lessing–Magnum) **33** (BP) **34** *Apotheosis of Prince Eugene* (Meyer) **35** (BP) **38–39** Bernardo Bellotto, *View of Vienna from the Belvedere*, 1759–60. KMV

CHAPTER 2 **43** Martin van Meytens II, *Maria Theresia and her Family*, 1750. Schoenbrunn Palace, Vienna (Meyer) **44** Joseph Haydn. HMSW **45** Pietro Metastasio. HMSW **46** Leaping Lippizaner. (Erich Lessing–Magnum) **47** Martin van Meytens II, *Damenkarousel*, 1750. Schoenbrunn Palace (Meyer) **48** (BP) **49** Millionen Room, Schoenbrunn. (Meyer) **50** Helbing, *Mozart*, 1768. Mozarteum, Salzburg **51** Lorenzo da Ponte. BONV **52** Mozart's *Requiem*. BONV (Erich Lessing – Magnum) **53** (BP) **54** Mozart, Piano Sonata in A Minor, K. 310. Private coll. **55** Joseph Lange, *Mozart*. Mozarteum, Salzburg **56** (BP) **58–59** Bacler d'Albe, *Bombing of Vienna*, 1809. Versailles

CHAPTER 3 **62** W.J. Mähler, *Beethoven*, 1815. Beethovenhaus, Bonn. **63** (BP) **64** top left Wilhelm Thöny, *Beethoven*. **65** top right Three Sonatas. All: Beethovenhaus, Bonn **64–65** bottom Lobkowitz Palace. HMSW **66** Joseph Danhauser, *Beethoven's Hands*, 1827. Beethovenhaus, Bonn **67** Theater an der Wien, (Marvin E. Newman) **68–69** J.B. Isabey, *Congress of Vienna*, 1815. Bibliothèque Nationale, Paris **70–71** Johann Hochle, *Ball in the Winter Riding School*, 1815. Albertina, Vienna **72–73** Leopold Kupelwieser, *The Expulsion of Adam and Eve from Paradise*, 1820. HMSW **76–77** All: (BP)

CHAPTER 4 **80** *Grand Galop*. HMSW **81** Theo Zasche, *Johann Strauss, II*. BONV **82–83** Strauss Memorial. (Marvin E. Newman) **84** A. Graf, *C.W. von Metternich*. BONV **85** Wilhelm Gause, *Franz Joseph*. BONV **86–87** Gustav Veith, *Bird's-eye View of Vienna*, 1873. HMSW **89** Main staircase of Vienna Opera. (Erich Lessing–Magnum) **90–91** Both: BONV **92–93** Wilhelm Gause, *Court Ball in Hofburg Palace*, 1890. HMSW

CHAPTER 5 **96** top left: Demel's und Sohne. (Adam Woolfitt–Woodfin Camp) **96–97** All: (BP) **99** Gustav Klimt, *Philosophy*. HMSW **101** Gustav Klimt, *Judith*, 1901. Austrian Gallery, Vienna (Meyer) **103** top: Artists of the 14th Secession Exhibition, 1902. BONV bottom (BP) **104** Gustav Mahler. BONV **106–107** Franz Alt, *The Ringstrasse*, ca. 1880. HMSW **109** Both: Sudd Verlag **110–111** Wilhelm Gause, *Mayor Karl Lueger in the Prater*. HMSW

CHAPTER 6 **115** top: Hans Makart, *Franz Joseph Leaving Hofburg Palace*, 1879. BONV bottom: Franz Ferdinand, Sarajevo, 1916. BONV **115** Franz Joseph, 1916. BONV **117** Both: BONV **118** Egon Schiele, *Paris von Gütersloh*, 1918. Minneapolis Institute of Arts, 1954. **119** Arnold Schoenberg 1951. BONV **120–21** Both: BONV **122** BONV **123** Joseph Weinheber, 1937. BONV **124–25** Both: BONV **126** Parliament. (Marvin E. Newman) **129** (BP) **130** Ernst Fuchs (Margos Pilz) **131** Ernst Fuchs, *Eva Christina*. Collection of the Artist. **132–35** All: (BP) **136** (BP)

VIENNA IN LITERATURE **139–60** Selection of illustrations from *Ver Sacrum*, Vienna, 1898–1903.
REFERENCE **164** Map of Vienna by Wilhelmina Reyinga.

Index